Grasping God's Purpose:

"Lessons from the Book of Exodus"

Volume One

Exodus 1:1 – 15:27

By Dr. Randall D. Smith

These volumes were prepared with students and teachers of the Bible in mind. The series is taken from the actual teaching notes of Dr. Smith as he teaches through all the books of the Bible each year at Great Commission Bible Institute in Sebring, Florida.

Lessons in Volume One

Lesson One: Exodus 1:1-2:10 "The Foundations of a Nation"

Key Principle: God may approve trouble in my life to bring out my choice to become obedient even when it's uncomfortable for me; yet He is good!

Lesson Two: Exodus 2:11 - 3:12 "The Source"

Key Principle: We cannot accomplish God's will in our strength and our plan – only in His time with His presence and His power.

Lesson Three: Exodus 3:1-10 "Tug of War"

Key Principle: God has set the pattern for how He calls men and women to service for Him - but we must understand the pattern and identify His call in our lives.

Lesson Four: Exodus 3:10-4:18 "Your identification, please!"

Key Principle: A believer's success in doing God's desires is not bounded by our abilities, but by our understanding of and submission to God's power.

Lesson Five: Exodus 4:14-31 "Heeding the Call"

Key Principle: God's people must be prepared to hear God's call and move at His direction. To do so, we must know how to respond appropriately.

Lesson Six: Exodus 4:27-5:23 "The Key to Success"

Key Principle: To a believer, success is whole-hearted obedience to the Word of God - regardless of any external outcomes.

Lesson Seven: Exodus 6:1-13 "God of the Open Door

Key Principle: The depth of your relationship with God is directly connected to the depth of what doors in your heart you open to Him!

Lesson Eight: Exodus 6:14-7:13 "The God that Will Be Known" (Part 1)

Key Principle: God wants people to know Him and to show others Who He is!

Lesson Nine: Exodus 7:14-11:10 "The God that Will Be Known" (Part 2)

Key Principle: When God is truly seen, men know the truth – they cannot trust any other beside Him.

Lesson Ten: Exodus 7-12 "The God that Will Be Known" (Part 3)

Key Principle: God is reaching out to men and women – but they must learn to see Him through the dust the world is kicking up around them!

Lesson Eleven: Exodus 12:1-28 "The Safe Combination"

Key Principle: God's acceptance is only on God's terms, no one else's opinion really matters!

Lesson Twelve: Exodus 13:1-21 "Take the Long Road Home"

Key Principle: God knows the short way is not always the best way to move us ahead. He takes His time to make sure the way we head is pleasing to Him!

Lesson Thirteen: Exodus 14:1-31 "A Choice Vessel"

Key Principle: To become a vessel God can use, I must understand and then live the choices that God will be honored by.

Lesson Fourteen: Exodus 15:1-27 "The Day after Syndrome"

Key Principle: I must learn Who God is and how He works in the journey to be able to both enjoy life and walk with Him.

Table of Contents

Grasping God's Purpose: Lessons in Exodus

Lesson One: Exodus 1-2:10
"The Foundations of a Nation"

When you read the stories of Moses and Israel, you have to marvel at the defiant, complaining, unappreciative ways of the Hebrews and then ask yourself how (or why) Moses ever stuck with them. Knowing myself, I would have been tempted to resign and send resumes to the Amorites, Jebusites or the other local "ites." Anyone in the need of a liberator? What I have never appreciated until recently was the significance of Israel being a community of ex-slaves with all the attitudes and default behaviors that result from 400 years of oppression.

As many years as I have known their story, it never occurred to me that when one generation after another has been denied essential human rights and lost its dignity, such people will become seriously impaired at making (solid) decisions, be loyal, trust leaders, hope for tomorrow, or even get along with each other…

"Leaders today may want to think about what characterizes people who enter the Christian community from lives of raw unbelief. That's what we have to look forward to in the coming years. Ours is no longer a Christianized society where most people come to us with a basic understanding of biblical ways and norms. The strengths and restraints of a strong community life no longer apply…" (*Gordon McDonald*)

Gordon was trying to frame a problem we grapple with in our church. As we reach out, new people are being led to Christ. They come into our midst and try to understand where we are when their whole world is different than the truths they hear from God's Word here. There is a man who struggled to reflect what God was doing in him, like many of you are right now…

Our series on Exodus begins with a question: Why does God allow punishing times of trouble in our lives? How can I say that God is good "all the time" when He sat back and watched His people be enslaved and beaten? What kind of God lets me go through hard times? What is His objective in such times?

Key Principle: God may approve trouble in my life to bring out my choice to become obedient even when it's uncomfortable for me; yet He is good!

Exodus opens in heartbreak. God had not left His people – in fact, He was blessing them in many ways. At the same time, they needed strength to get through a difficult and painful, but formative experience in their history. As with so many Bible stories, the work of God is set on a canvas of struggle.

First, recognize the page had turned from the generation that we have been studying in Genesis. The fathers may have had profound lessons of faith etched in their faces, but they were gone now.

Exodus 1:1 Now these are the names of the sons of Israel who came to Egypt with Jacob; they came each one with his household: 2 Reuben, Simeon, Levi and Judah; 3 Issachar, Zebulun and Benjamin; 4 Dan and Naphtali, Gad and Asher. 5 All the persons who came from the loins of Jacob were seventy in number, but Joseph was already in Egypt. 6 Joseph died, and all his brothers and all that generation.

Second, we must understand that God's leftover blessing in keeping His Word to Abraham, Isaac, and Jacob was met in the world with deep resentment and suspicion.

Exodus 1:7 But the sons of Israel were fruitful and increased greatly, and multiplied, and became exceedingly mighty, so that the land was filled with them. 8 Now a new king arose over Egypt, who did not know Joseph. 9 He said to his people, "Behold, the people of the sons of Israel are more and mightier than we. 10 Come, let us deal wisely with them, or else they will multiply and in the event of war, they will also join themselves to those who hate us, and fight against us and depart from the land." 11 So they appointed taskmasters over them to afflict them with hard labor. And they built for Pharaoh storage cities, Pithom and Raamses. 12 But the more they afflicted them, the more they multiplied and the more they spread out, so that they were in dread of the sons of Israel. 13 The Egyptians compelled the sons of

Israel to labor rigorously; 14 and they made their lives bitter with hard labor in mortar and bricks and at all kinds of labor in the field, all their labors which they rigorously imposed on them.

Each time we study God's Word closely, we see a canvas of struggle on which God paints His story.

Here is a question we must ask: "Why does God allow punishing times of trouble in our lives?" I mean, how can we honestly say that God is good "all the time" when He sat back and watched His people be enslaved and beaten? What kind of God lets us go through hard times? What are His objectives in such times? That is the purpose of this book called "Exodus" – to explain the purposes of God to a young generation of believers. Before we can go very far into the book, we must acknowledge an unchanging truth - God may approve trouble in our lives to bring out our choice to become obedient even when it's uncomfortable for us, yet He is good!

There are seven principles to keep in mind during the process of 'Painful Separation:'

Note the progression of the text...

First, there is what could be called the "purpose principle":

Being IN the world and not OF the world is a question of purpose. (1 John chapters 2 and 3 call us to work in the world but not to love the things of the world.) God's people came to the world to be a testimony and an influence, but overstayed their purpose in that place (1:1-8). They started with a godly purpose: God promised to reunite Jacob to his son and for God bringing the evil of Joseph's brothers to "good" for the world and for the believers (1:1-6).

Second, we might refer to the "comfort principle":

Prosperity moved in and the people forgot their original call to be a distinct people in their homeland. They grew in number, but also in power and influence. All this satisfied them (1:7). When the people of God become closely identified with the culture they live in and don't live as they are called to be distinct, they are infected by the same cultural maladies of the rest of the lost world!

Third, there is what appears to be the "faithfulness principle":

God is faithful to His promises and finishes what He starts. Even in disobedience, there is preservation. A closer look at verse 12 makes that clear! God's plan for His children is **not over when they overstay their time**. They didn't belong there! **God approved a trouble to move them back to obedience: A king overtook Pharaoh's** household and troubles descended on Egypt that affected the people of God (1:8-11). God blesses in spite of the conditions to preserve His covenant and cause (1:12).

Fourth, we may observe a "pain principle":

Pain is a positive tool in the hands of a God Who has not been obeyed. It is a natural teacher, and causes us to reflect even when we resist reflection normally! If we will **not** separate ourselves from the world, God may use the world to separate them from us. It is a painful process, but can be avoided by obedience (1:13-14).

Fifth, there appears to be a "membership principle":

This world is not your home; it is a place to journey through to get to your home. We bring blessing into it, but must be careful to see it for what it is (cp. 1 Cor. 7). Remember the world has no true interest in you. They will rob you of your strength and use you to further their objectives. The blessing you bring will be siphoned off for their best interest (1:15-16).

Exodus 1:15 Then the king of Egypt spoke to the Hebrew midwives, one of whom was named Shiphrah and the other was named Puah; 16 and he said, "When you are helping the Hebrew women to give birth and see them upon the birthstool, if it is a son, then you shall put him to death; but if it is a daughter, then she shall live."

Sixth, there is something that may be called the "standing principle":

It is better to stand for the next truth even though you failed on previous truths.

Exodus 1:17 But the midwives feared God, and did not do as the king of Egypt had commanded them, but let the boys live. 18 So the king of Egypt called for the midwives and said to them, "Why have you done this thing, and let the boys live?" 19 The midwives said to Pharaoh, "Because the Hebrew women are not as the Egyptian women; for they are vigorous and give birth before the midwife can get to them." 20 So God was good to the midwives, and the people multiplied, and became very mighty. 21 Because the midwives feared God, He established households for them.

Because this world is not our home, we must constantly be reminded that this is a place to journey through to get to your home. Even when caught in the world, do not forget who you are and **to Whom** you belong. Faithfulness will have its own rewards, and compromise its own calamity (1:17-21). Compounding wrongs is NOT the way forward!

Seventh, there appears to be a "non-negotiable principle":

To live without compromising your values, you must work hard to be submissive, have great sensitivity, and sometimes creativity. Yet you cannot abandon your principles. The world will take ownership of any good thing you bring to them. They will not consider your God or His blessings, but will only become defensive. They will ask you to compromise more and more (1:22-2:3), and time spent with them will become harder and harder. Remember, you are in this situation because of choices to make yourself at home with them!

Exodus 1:22 Then Pharaoh commanded all his people, saying, "Every son who is born you are to cast into the Nile, and every daughter you are to keep alive." 2:1 Now a man from the house of Levi went and married a daughter of Levi.

2 The woman conceived and bore a son; and when she saw that he was beautiful, she hid him for three months. 3 But when she could hide him no longer, she got him a wicker basket and covered it over with tar and pitch. Then she put the child into it and set it among the reeds by the bank of the Nile.

If we keep reading our story, we will find that the women who stood up to Pharaoh were only an element of a larger story. **God was about to send an answer to the needs of His people. He used, as before, a woman of strength and courage. Look at the story:**

Exodus 2:4 His sister stood at a distance to find out what would happen to him. 5 The daughter of Pharaoh came down to bathe at the Nile, with her maidens walking alongside the Nile; and she saw the basket among the reeds and sent her maid, and she brought it to her. 6 When she opened it, she saw the child, and behold, the boy was crying. And she had pity on him and said, "This is one of the Hebrews' children." 7 Then his sister said to Pharaoh's daughter, "Shall I go and call a nurse for you from the Hebrew women that she may nurse the child for you?" 8 Pharaoh's daughter said to her, "Go ahead." So the girl went and called the child's mother. 9 Then Pharaoh's daughter said to her, "Take this child away and nurse him for me and I will give you your wages." So the woman took the child and nursed him. 10 The child grew, and she brought him to Pharaoh's daughter and he became her son. And she named him Moses, and said, "Because I drew him out of the water."

Look at Jochebed (we know her name and her husband Amram from Exodus 6). What do you see?

She was a grounded woman:

I see a woman with a godly heritage from the words of *Exodus 2:1: Now a man from the house of Levi went and married a daughter of Levi.*

It is worth reminding ourselves that we must never underestimate the benefit of a godly heritage. I want to mention that some of you did not come from a home where both parents were saved. It may be you were raised like Timothy in 2 Timothy 1:5 by a godly grandma and mom. It is always best if all the players are followers of Jesus, but it is not essential, merely helpful!

She was a committed woman:

I see a woman who made the **commitment of marriage** (2:1 married a daughter of Levi). **The commitment to each other before God precedes the commitment to a child's welfare** – this is strongest.

James Dobson tells about a time he came home when his son, Ryan, was a small baby. It had been a terrible day for his wife. Ryan had been sick, and had cried all day long. Once, as she was changing his diapers, the telephone rang & Shirley reached over to answer it before fastening up his diapers. Just then Ryan had an attack of diarrhea. She cleaned up that mess and put him in clean, sweet-smelling clothes. Then she took him into the living room and fed him. As she was burping him he threw up all over himself, her, and the couch, too. Dobson writes, "When I came home I could smell the aroma of motherhood everywhere." Shirley cried out to him, "Was all of this in my contract?" What kind of person does this? The committed kind!

She was a loving woman:

I see a woman who was **in love with her child**. In Exodus 2:2, *she "gazed at" the child:* The woman conceived and bore a son; and when she saw that he was beautiful, she hid him for three months.

She was a careful woman:

I see a woman who was **hopeful and not impulsive**. Ex. 2:2 *ends with* "hid him for three months." *She worked on a hopeful plan.*

Ex. 2:3 But when she could hide him no longer, she got him a wicker basket and covered it over with tar and pitch. Then she put the child into it and set it among the reeds by the bank of the Nile.

Remember the image of Titus 2:5 "workers at home" can also be translated "protectors of the home." The image of the lioness on the steps at the front door of the house is appropriate here.

She was a tested woman:

Look at *Exodus 2:9 Then Pharaoh's daughter said to her, "Take this child away and nurse him for me and I will give you your wages." So the woman took the child and nursed him. 10 The child grew, and she brought him to Pharaoh's daughter and he became her son. And she named him Moses, and said, "Because I drew him out of the water."*

God placed two stages in parenting: **protection** and then **preparation**. As preparation increases, protection decreases. The balancing act on this is not precise. There are times you will protect when you should prepare. Don't worry; eventually they will cut loose. The hard part is preparing THEM and YOU for the cut of the apron strings!

All the big guns of the enemy are aimed at the home. The moral issues of our time are derived to a great extent from poor homes. **Simply put, the best way you can build a strong America is build a strong home. The best way you can change your neighborhood is change your home. Are you up to the task? We dare not forget that strong children are most often constructed by strong mothers.**

Jochebed had learned that though she lived in a time of great trouble and suffering, God called her to be obedient even when it was uncomfortable. Her faithfulness to God instilled in the life of her son Moses the quality God was to use in future years to bring her people out of slavery.

For the believer, life is not about comfort; it is not about fulfillment; it is not about fitting in. Life is short and about pleasing my Master, who gave Himself for me. God may approve trouble in our lives to bring out our choice to become obedient even when it's uncomfortable for us, yet He is good!

Grasping God's Purpose: Lessons in Exodus

Lesson Two: Exodus 2:11-3:12 "The Source"

In 1965, James A. Michener published a historical novel called *The Source*. The novel acts as a survey of the history of the Jewish people from antiquity and their meager beginnings to the modern State of Israel. Set at a fictional tell (mound or ruin) in northern Israel called "Makor" (Hebrew: "source"), the story is interwoven with two time frames – a story set in modern-day Israel laid over an ancient historical timeline. As archaeologists dig Makor, they expose artifacts, allowing the author to journey off into the lives of the people involved with that artifact long before. The book traces a fictional beginning of monotheism, weaving in details of biblical characters like David and his kingdom, as well as Jews of Hellenistic and Roman times, etc. Makor is traced through the period of the Crusades and its final destruction by the Mameluks (circa. 1291) and is not rebuilt by the Ottomans.

This telling offers not only a graphic depiction of the land and its history – but also its people. The source of the author's story is the physical site, but that isn't the real source of the people of Israel – that is found in a different book. That story is dramatically captured in the book of Exodus.

Our last lesson raised the question: "Why does God allow punishing times of trouble in our lives?" Today, we move to a second question – **"How can God really use me?"** To be even more precise, our passage addresses, **"What do I need to accomplish God's plan for me?"**

Between verse 10 and verse 11 nearly 40 years are passed over in silence. The account in Exodus throws no light on the nearly 40 years Moses spent in the courts of Egypt. According to Acts 7:23 *when Moses was forty years old, it came into his heart to visit his brethren the children of Israel.*

Thus, as we continue our study, we move from the baby Moses, set in a basket and floating into the court of Pharaoh, to Moses the man. He grew up in two worlds – a Hebrew slave child educated and privileged above his peers to be a prince of Egypt. Within his conflicted identity, we can see all the passion of a man who desires to do right, but falls flat in his attempts. We know the end of the story, for we read it with full knowledge of the man's later greatness. Yet, if we place ourselves back into his life, things weren't nearly so clear.

Moses was a troubled man – divided in loyalties and hotheaded in temperament. Knowing the right thing is not enough to accomplishing God's plan in your life. Having good ideas and goals is not enough. In the end, an encounter with God reveals the essential source for accomplishing God's will in our lives.

Key Principle: We cannot accomplish God's will in our strength and our plan – only in His time with His presence and His power.

As we look at the story more closely, we find there are two parts to the narrative. The first is what Moses DID – working in his own strength. The second part is how God RESPONDED – and rehabilitated the man of God after he failed.

Part One: The "Self-Strength" Failure – Drawing from my "self" source. (2:11-15)

The passage opens with seven events that led Moses to an end in his own strength. Moses had POSITION and POWER. At the same time, without the proper source to draw from, Moses was USELESS when it came to doing God's will. The stages of failure depending on self are neither unique nor uncommon – so they are well worth examining up close:

First, Identity Conflict: Moses felt the division of living in two worlds – a Hebrew heritage and an Egyptian education (2:11a).

Exodus 2:11 Now it came about in those days, when Moses had grown up, that he went out to his brethren and looked on their hard labors…

Not to spiritualize this point, but every person in this room has felt this kind of conflict. When the enemy wants to knock you off track, he starts by making you feel different than others around you. Before some he dangles the idea of entitlement. Before others he captures them in the idea that they are victims. Still others he simply offers a puffed up pride, whispering in their ear. We must respond well – for that is our responsibility. At the same time, never underestimate the power of the enemy's whisper.

Second, Anger Triggers: An event flamed his passion - in the face of injustice his emotions took control (2:11b).

Exodus 2:11b … and he saw an Egyptian beating a Hebrew, one of his brethren.

Our weakness is most often associated with our emotional vulnerability. We see something or hear something that upset us, and the emotions begin to steal the blood flow from the reasoned part of our brain. We start to react, rather than respond.

Third, Self-Reliance: He used his own strength to conquer the injustice in a wrong act (2:12).

Exodus 2:12 So he looked this way and that, and when he saw there was no one around, he struck down the Egyptian and hid him in the sand.

It is tempting to think that as Moses witnessed the abuse to his fellow Hebrew that something just snapped. But scripture portrays that this was all a part of a preconceived plan on the part of Moses. He decided that it was time to take action so according to verse 12 of our text, *he looked this way and that way, and when he saw no one, he killed the Egyptian and hid him in the sand.* He looked this way and that but unfortunately he never looked up.

He knew God's will - but he did not really know God well! He did not bother to seek God's way in God's time. The problem is when we understand what God's will for our lives is, but things are not happening fast enough to suit us, we become anxious. We try to give God a hand.

When Moses stepped in to begin his own "Operation Deliverance," he was energized by the flesh not by the Spirit and call of God. Here is the crux of the issue – he relied on his hastily made plan, incubated in the flash of anger. He neither sought, nor did he accept alternative plans. He thought of something and he acted. That may have the raw marks of a potential leader, but in untested hands, it is nothing short of destructive and dangerous.

Fourth, Self-Justification: He slept on it. It seems he felt his cause justified his actions – might made right (a reflection of exactly how the Egyptian rationalized the slave beating! 2:13a).

Exodus 2:13 He went out the next day…

We have an incredible ability to feel right about doing wrong. We set up ever- moving standards of right and wrong. We sleep on things when we should lay awake absolutely broken over our heart condition!

Fifth, Guilt: He faced guilt and shame when he was discovered – the buried rationalization no longer felt sufficient. (2:13b-14).

Exodus 2:13b …and behold, two Hebrews were fighting with each other; and he said to the offender, "Why are you striking your companion?" 14 But he said, "Who made you a prince or a judge over us? Are you intending to kill me as you killed the Egyptian?" Then Moses was afraid and said, "Surely the matter has become known."

When our deeds are brought to light, our rationalized logic looks really, well, dumb. We see what we did through the light of the day, and it doesn't look good. Guilt eats up our strength and fear dominates every thought.

Sixth, Flight: He fled from punishment (2:15a).

Exodus 2:15a When Pharaoh heard of this matter, he tried to kill Moses. But Moses fled from the presence of Pharaoh and settled in the land of Midian…

Self-preservation is God-given, but irresponsibility is not. Moses was a big man when he had the power, but he wasn't about to face the consequences of his actions if he could out-run the law. Consider how different he was than Joseph, the other Hebrew–Egyptian prince.

Seventh, Exhaustion: He ended the story slumped over and exhausted (2:15b).

Exodus 2:15b: …and he sat down by a well.

To live on the run is absolutely exhausting. To run from your past, you have to take pains to cover your tracks. The number of places you cannot go grows, and life is about staying in the shadows. It wasn't necessarily because you had all the wrong values; it may have been that you tried to do things in your own strength and according to your own plan.

Part Two: God's Rehabilitation Plan (2:16-3:12)

It is ironic that God turned the whole story at a well! Look at the stages God used to draw Moses from a position of power and uselessness to a position of powerlessness and usefulness. In 2:16-3:1 we can see how God prepared Moses because his plan didn't work. Instead, God grabbed his heart and transformed the man. How did that happen?

God used his exhaustion - waited until Moses was backed into his own corner before He introduced Moses to his future life (2:16).

Exodus 2:16 Now the priest of Midian had seven daughters; and they came to draw water and filled the troughs to water their father's flock.

There simply is no point to God trying to work in a man until the man has seen the end of self-effort. His own failures and the exhaustion of toiling labors are often the platform of God's work in Him!

God used his character – God drew him in based on his sense of injustice (2:17).

Exodus 2:17 Then the shepherds came and drove them away, but Moses stood up and helped them and watered their flock.

God didn't call Moses to do something that was not planted deep within the chords of his personal passions. God used the man's nature to pull him into service and guide him along the path to his life mission.

God used old friends – God guided Moses by introducing him to people who knew God well (2:18-21).

Exodus 2:18 When they came to Reuel their father, he said, "Why have you come back so soon today?" 19 So they said, "An Egyptian delivered us from the hand of the shepherds, and what is more, he even drew the water for us and watered the flock." 20 He said to his daughters, "Where is he then? Why is it that you have left the man behind? Invite him to have something to eat." 21 Moses was willing to dwell with the man, and he gave his daughter Zipporah to Moses.

When God wanted to draw Moses, he used people that already knew God. Moses may not have encountered God Himself until the burning bush, but he was already living in the encampment of other believers (i.e. "friend of God"). For many of us, we meet God's friends on our way to our meeting with God Himself.

God used his circumstances – God placed Moses into a molding place where life circumstances did a work on him.

Exodus 2:22 Then she gave birth to a son, and he named him Gershom, for he said, "I have been a sojourner in a foreign land." (child responsibilities).

Exodus 3:1 Now Moses was pasturing the flock of Jethro his father-in-law, the priest of Midian; and he led the flock to the west side of the wilderness and came to Horeb, the mountain of God. (tenderness and faithfulness).

Though surrounded by believers, God also used a series of life lessons that come best by experiences. He used childbirth and allowed Moses to feel both the thrill and responsibility of fatherhood. He used countless hours of tending a flock in harsh conditions to pattern a leader's faithfulness and tender care of the helpless.

God crafted His plan – behind the scenes God was listening and building the players to bring about His plan (2:23-25)

Exodus 2:23 Now it came about in the course of those many days that the king of Egypt died. And the sons of Israel sighed because of the bondage, and they cried out; and their cry for help because of their bondage rose up to God. 24 So God heard their groaning; and God remembered His covenant with Abraham, Isaac, and Jacob. 25 God saw the sons of Israel, and God took notice of them.

History was being crafted by God apart from Moses. He was watching, listening, and exposing His plan – piece by piece. Moses wasn't aware of where God was leading him, nor was he fully aware of what was going on back in Egypt. **God was weaving together the questions of His people and God's prepared answer – but neither side knew the other.**

There came a point in the story where God moved in and began overtly directing Moses- a time of enlistment to serve (3:2-12). It is interesting to see exactly what God used to grab hold of Moses:

God acted with extraordinary (God-sized) Patience: God encountered the man when the man was ready to meet (3:2).

Exodus 3:2 The angel of the LORD appeared to him in a blazing fire from the midst of a bush; and he looked, and behold, the bush was burning with fire, yet the bush was not consumed.

God used a point of attraction: God got his attention through some event apart fro*m his expectation (3:3)*

Exodus 3:3 So Moses said, "I must turn aside now and see this marvelous sight, why the bush is not burned up."

God tailored the message: God spoke directly into his heart in a personal way (3:4).

Exodus 3:4 When the LORD saw that he turned aside to look God called to him from the midst of the bush and said, "Moses, Moses!" And he said, "Here I am."

This is an important observation recorded in the text. Moses grew up well (palace life), but one day went to see what hardship his people were enduring. (2:11a). It can be deeply powerful to see first-hand the pain of others when you have lived a privileged and sheltered life (2:11b) and God used that encounter to cement a need in his heart and help define his call...Consider this: Every follower of God has an assignment that He has placed in your life, and believe it or not, often the movement of your heart toward something is the key to reveal what it is to you. You may know your gifting, but it will be your "**hunger**" that will often reveal your assignment on Earth.

- The teacher must long to conquer ignorance.
- For a doctor to spend many years in medical school he must long to see sick people made well.
- A good lawyer must burn within and despise injustice.

- A good missionary must ache over the thought of people dying and missing eternity with God.

Here is a tip that may be helpful: Find out what makes you tick, so you can handle what ticks you off.

The irritation of injustice or the burden of some particular unsolved problem may actually offer an indicator to your call by God!

Stop for a moment at each step of the passage as you continue your study. Continue to note how God dealt with Moses – it is enlightening!

God made clear the man's sinfulness and God's holiness (5:5-6)

Exodus 3:5 Then He said, "Do not come near here; remove your sandals from your feet, for the place on which you are standing is holy ground." 6 He said also, "I am the God of your father, the God of Abraham, the God of Isaac, and the God of Jacob." Then Moses hid his face, for he was afraid to look at God.

That is a foundational place for a call is clarified into reality. God doesn't call us because we are GOOD or ABLE – but because He chose to use us. When we begin any venture with the knowledge of our weakness, it builds meekness into our walk.

God laid out the call by offering a burden (3:7-9)

Exodus 3:7 The LORD said, "I have surely seen the affliction of My people who are in Egypt, and have given heed to their cry because of their taskmasters, for I am aware of their sufferings. 8 So I have come down to deliver them from the power of the Egyptians, and to bring them up from that land to a good and spacious land, to a land flowing with milk and honey, to the place of the Canaanite and the Hittite and the Amorite and the Perizzite and the Hivite and the Jebusite. 9 Now, behold, the cry of the sons of

Israel has come to Me; furthermore, I have seen the oppression with which the Egyptians are oppressing them."

God will not bless the plan He has not designed. Because we justify our actions does not mean they are right, nor that others will see them as we do. Initially, Moses probably did not see himself as a murderer but as one striking the first blow for the freedom of God's people. Bottom line: Moses' plans are not the same plans made by God for the deliverance of the Hebrews. When God offered HIS BURDEN, light fell on the plan of the Divine to use His servant.

God personally enlisted Moses to join His work (10).

Exodus 3:10 Therefore, come now, and I will send you to Pharaoh, so that you may bring My people, the sons of Israel, out of Egypt.

F.B. Meyers gives a wonderful assessment when he wrote, "Such experiences come to us all. We rush forward, thinking to carry all before us; we strike a few blows in vain; we are staggered with disappointment and reel back; we are afraid at the first breath of human disapproval; we flee from the scenes of our discomfiture to hide ourselves in chagrin. Then we are hidden in the secret of God's presence from the pride of man. And there our vision clears; the silt drops from the current of our life; our self-life dies down; our spirit drinks of the river of God, which is full of water; our faith begins to grasp His arm and to be the channel for the manifestation of His power; and thus at last we emerge to be His hand to lead an exodus." (F. B. Meyer. Lance Wubbels, ed. *The Life of Moses,* Lynnwood, Washington: Emerald Books, 1996 p. 30)

God offered the secret to the success of the venture – a pledge of divine presence (3:11-12).

Exodus 3:11 But Moses said to God, "Who am I, that I should go to Pharaoh, and that I should bring the sons of Israel out of Egypt?" 12 And He said, "Certainly I will be with you, and this shall be the sign to you that it is I who have sent you: when you have brought the people out of Egypt, you shall worship God at this mountain."

The morning Moses met God, only God knew it would happen. To Moses, it was another day of loneliness on the back side of defeat. Although at times we may "feel" like we are alone in our wilderness experiences we are not.

"Whether you have known it or not, felt it or not, even believed it or not, God has not taken His hand off your life....It is dry. It is lonely. You feel dismal and sad. But whatever your emotions may be telling you, the Bible says you not alone." (Charles Swindoll, *Moses: A Man of Selfless Dedication*, Nashville: Word, 1999 pp. 76, 77)

We cannot accomplish God's will in our strength and our plan – only in His time with His presence and His power. Remember, God is capable of working for us and in us, in spite of us.

Moses the man who botched things so badly on his own was used mightily of God. His name is mentioned 700 times in the Bible. He was used by God in a greater way than any other Old Testament character, when he, through failure, learned to follow God's plans rather than his own.

When I was seven years old, my family was forced out of our home because of a legal technicality. I had to work to help support my family. At age nine, while still a backwards, shy little boy, my mother died. At age 22, I lost my job as a store clerk. I wanted to go to law school but my education wasn't good enough. At 23, I went into debt to become a partner in a small store. Three years later my partner died leaving me a huge debt, which took years to repay. At 28, after developing romantic relations with a young lady for four years, I asked her to marry me. She said, "No." At 37, on my third try, I was finally elected to the United States Congress. Two years later, I ran again and failed to be re-elected. I had a nervous breakdown at that time. At 41, adding additional heartache to an already unhappy marriage, my four-year-old son died. The next year I ran for Land Officer and lost. At 45, I ran for the Senate and lost. A few years later, I ran for the Vice-Presidency and lost. At 49, I ran for the Senate again and lost. And at 51, I was elected President of the United States. Who am I? My name is Abraham Lincoln.

Grasping God's Purpose: Lessons in Exodus

Lesson Three: Exodus 3:1-10 "Tug of War"

We have all played the game. It isn't complicated. Two teams form and grab two ends of a rope. The rope has a knot in the middle, and that knot is positioned over the starting point, so that neither side gets an unfair advantage in the beginning. Each side will pull desperately to try to drag the other team across the center line. When one side has successfully pulled the opposing team across the line, the pulling team wins. It is even better if the center is a muddy and messy pit! The game is simple, but very old. According to a book from the Tang Imperial Dynasty of China (C7th -10th CE), tug of war (under the name "hook pulling") was used by the military commander of the State of Chu in east central China to train warriors. Emperor Xuanzong of Tang held large-scale tug of war games, using ropes of five hundred feet with shorter ropes attached and more than five hundred people on each end of the rope. Each side positioned a team of drummers to encourage the participants.

Maybe you haven't played at that scale – few of us have. At the same time, many believers are playing a huge "tug of war" with God on a daily basis. We want to live for Him, but we want to have what we want at the same time – and that causes a tension. We believe He knows what is best for us, but we seem unable to really get it done in our daily life. Still others seem paralyzed, hoping that God's specific will in their lives will somehow be miraculously clarified. It is time for us to address the will of God and His call in your life *again*. It is time to reopen the call of Moses for another look…

.

Key Principle: God's call is not mystical. He has set the pattern for how He calls men and women to service for Him – but we must understand the pattern and identify His call in our lives.

Our passage offers ten principles for God's call that may help you on your journey to define direction, based on the model of Moses' life:

First, note that God calls those who are already faithful in the things He has given them to do (3:1a).

We cannot choose to be walking in sin and self and still be ready to meet God. Erwin MacManus wrote: "In Christianity, the goal of the spiritual journey is the transformation of our desires." Wow! What a powerful statement!

Exodus 3:1 Now Moses was pasturing the flock of Jethro his father-in-law, the priest of Midian...

Moses was busy doing the right thing when God met him. If you do what you know God has told you to do today, you are walking in God's will. It is better to try to tame a wild stallion than to ride a dead horse – so we need to be moving ahead NOW in what we know to do. God works with those in motion. It is important to note that God will clarify your journey in the midst of obedience – not beforehand.... Wake up! Get out of bed! God wants to change the world through your life if you will just get busy following Him. God is busy reducing our desires down to a single desire – to follow Him.

We need to resign the need to have provision before vision. We need to lay down the idea that God should explain the importance of every acts of obedience to us in order to get us to follow today. Some acts of faithfulness are not going to be explained. They will put you in the right frame of mind, or even the right place at the right time for God to do something incredible – but you won't get a guarantee on that beforehand. Clean the toilet with the knowledge that if you have been given the latrine assignment by God, you must do it the best you can – so that God can use it for His glory.

Second, God's call is most often found when we are in places associated with God's voice (3:1b).

God can speak anywhere, but He has some places that are common for communication with men – so choose where you spend your time

.
Exodus 3:1b ...and he led the flock to the west side of the wilderness and came to Horeb, the mountain of God.

When you move with God, He always shows up. If you spend time where He is known to frequent, the opportunities to hear His whisper increase dramatically. Psalm 1 says it so very well:

Psalm 1:1 How blessed is the man who does not walk in the counsel of the wicked nor stands in the path of sinners, nor sit in the seat of scoffers! 2 But his delight is in the law of the LORD, and in His law he meditates day and night.

Here is the point: A stable and mature life for God begins with discernment over where I must choose to build my life. Listen to the Psalmist's choices:

Does not walk (holek: from hawlak, to pass by and notice, to make one's periodic walk through) *in the counsel* (b'ay-tsaw' –in the advice) *of the wicked* (raw-shaw' – morally condemned or criminal). The desire for mature stability in the Lord makes me deliberately focus my view. I must interpret life based on His Word, and not succumb to the temptation of heeding the siren's song of those who are morally adrift. Moral truth and guidance comes from those who know God and walk with God – not those who I encounter along the path of life that have no such connection.

We live in a world of prodigal sons and daughters. In his book, *Balancing the Tightrope,* Barry Powell relates "in a survey of 200,000+ college freshmen, 76% listed financial prosperity as the most important of their life goals. Is it any wonder that one of the top issues in almost every presidential election is the economy? What has it come to when our top voting priority is our buying power? - even more important than crime, foreign policy or moral values. You see, like the prodigal son in Jesus' parable, we can buy into this world's mind set and make the same mistake he did: that life really does consist in the things that we possess." We must be careful to challenge that thinking and not buy into it.

Note the phrase *"Does not stand"* (awmad – to take one's stand in or characteristically build thought patterns) *in the path* (derech- the way or characteristic actions of) *of sinners* (chata'im – those who miss the mark and thereby offend). The desire for mature stability in the Lord causes me to dismiss opportunities to define life by the actions of the crowd who routinely offend God. My standard cannot be found there! I dare not pause too long and ponder their ways, nor do I take my stand on the basis of their actions.

Do not misunderstand. God still values the person who is making all the wrong choices, but we are not to take our stand among them. Holiness cannot be transmitted by osmosis, but corruption can (Haggai 2:10-13) – so we need to be warned.

A well-known speaker started off his seminar by holding up a $20 bill. In the room of over 200 people, he asked the question, "Who would like this $20 bill?" Hands started going up. He said, "I am going to give this $20 to one of you but first, let me do this." He proceeded to crumple the $20 dollar bill up. He then asked, "Who still wants it?" Still the hands were up in the air. "Well," he replied, "What if I do this?" And he dropped it on the ground and started to grind it into the floor with his shoe. He picked it up, now all crumpled and dirty. "Now who still wants it?" Still the hands were up in the air. "My friends, you have all learned a very valuable lesson. Because it did not decrease in value, it is still worth $20. Many times in our lives, we are dropped, crumpled, and ground into the dirt by the decisions we make and the circumstances that come our way. We feel as though we are worthless. But no matter what has happened or what will happen, you will never lose your value in God's eyes. To Him, dirty or clean, crumpled or finely creased, you are still priceless to Him." You see, it did not matter to the people sitting in that room that the $20 bill was dirty, crumpled, torn and worn down. (*sermon central illustrations*)

The issue isn't the value of the lost person; it is the placement of the yielded one. Do not spend too long in the world's way of thinking – trouble will result.

The text of the Psalm continues: *Does not sit* (yawshab – to take a seat or dwell comfortably) *in the seat* (moshawv – the dwelling place) *of scoffers* (loots – one who derides or mocks). The desire for mature stability in the Lord presses me so that I cannot become comfortable with dwelling among people who have no love for God and His Word. I must keep my distance from those who openly mock Him or what He has done.

Step away from the first verse and do not allow yourself to become uncomfortable with the negative nature of the words. In them is LIFE. God makes clear that our walk with Him will produce a happy and mature stability – but it comes at a price. We must choose not to follow those who have made their choice for a path that is NOT meant to honor Him. Some friendships that draw us into darkness must be courteously curtailed until we have the strength of the Spirit to renew them and bring to them a real comfort and example of the love of God. This cannot be done without grace, but we must be strong enough to stand in a windstorm before we venture into it. Many a testimony has been ruined by one who went into the storm without the proper strengthening – and the testimony was eroded rather than enhanced.

Every choice to spend time in an activity is a choice to deny spending time in all others.

It is not intrinsically a negative thought – it is a simple truth. We will not become stable, mature and happy in our walk with God if we do not limit the places our feet take us. Look carefully at your life. How are you being influenced? The opportunities to stop and pay attention to the world's wisdom abounds. The checkout stand in the local market promises to offer techniques on how to look like a movie star and "make our man or woman scream in ecstasy" in the bedroom. Horoscopes promise wisdom from the stars. Talk-show hosts promise us the answer to everything from politics to personal hygiene. Everyone knows how WE can be successful – even if they can't stay married while they give us the advice.

Now the positive - A stable and mature life for God is built on recalling and drawing from the truth God has revealed.

Psalm. 1:2 But his delight (khay'-fets does mean care or favor, but comes from an agricultural root word for the "bend" of a branch; a repositioning that allowed the branch to get best light and be most productive) is in the law (to-raw' – the term for the LAW is actually from an archer's term for an aimed shot; it was also used of a bullock, who set the way of the furrow) of the LORD, and in His law he meditates (yeh-geh is from daw-gaw' – to utter or devise a plan from) day and night.

We are not without a place to get truth. The world has their experts – we have the revealed truth of the Living God! When we deliberate our decisions based on its light and aim to hit the target of its principles our devised plan brings a result that honors our Master. Regardless of the results in this life, from the eternal perspective the desire to honor and delight the Lord has its own result. Did you notice that word "delight." It means to be "bent toward" something. Are we bent toward the Word for our answers?

1 Peter 2:2-3 reminds*: As newborn babes, desire the sincere milk of the word that you may grow thereby: If so be ye have tasted that the Lord is gracious.*

Our appetite for the Lord and His Word becomes quite dull when we have eaten too much of this world. We are satiated by the wrong things, and our hunger for good food has been displaced by the world's sugar-laden sauces.

Third, God's call begins with us meeting HIM, not simply HIS PLAN (3:2-3).

We need *Him*, not simply a key to the future. His presence is our key. Doors open as we approach them because we are walking with Him. The relationship precedes the path of direction.

Exodus 3:2 The angel of the LORD appeared to him in a blazing fire from the midst of a bush; and he looked, and behold, the bush was burning with fire, yet the bush was not consumed. 3 So Moses said, "I must turn aside now and see this marvelous sight, why the bush is not burned up."

The most important aspect of following God is spending time getting to know Him. You will never figure out His paths, but you can know His person. We need to be certain from His Word what He did and did not promise. We can know Him. We can walk with Him, but we do not lead Him – We follow Him. By definition, that means He calls the direction, not us. Know Him – and keep your eyes on Him – and let Him lead.

Fourth, when we respond to God's tug, He answers with more information (3:4a).

God won't pull us through the "dance" without our responding to His leadership. Look at the text:

Exodus 3:4 When the LORD saw that he turned aside to look, God called to him from the midst of the bush and said, "Moses, Moses!

"One of the greatest differences between the world's message about success and God's is this: **The world seeks a single formula to produce one set of results for all people, while God's plan is far more creative, far more individualized, and far more personal**. Moses did not have a vision for success early in his life, although as an adopted son of Pharaoh he enjoyed a certain degree of privilege. After murdering an Egyptian, however, he ran for his life and then spent forty years tending sheep. But one day the Lord revealed Himself to Moses and gave him a specific life mission. Many of us go through difficult and even devastating experiences, and then one day come face-to-face with the reality of God. Is this the pattern that God seems to be implementing in your life? If so, stick with His plan, regardless of how unorthodox it may seem. The Promised Land lies in that direction!" (*The Charles F. Stanley Life Principles Bible*)

Who can mistake the point: "Is not the essence of spiritual leadership someone who is willing to follow God first and closest?" (MacManus)

Fifth, when God calls, He expects an answer! (3:4b).

Putting off an answer is a sign of disrespect and disinterested callousness. Moses responded when he heard the voice:

Exodus 3:4b "...and he said, "Here I am."

One thing that made my parents crazy was when I ignored them. I found out early in my marriage the same thing about my wife. People want to know when you hear them – or they feel disrespected and unimportant. In that same way, God expects us to respect and acknowledge His call.

Sixth, recognition of God's Holiness is required before we can follow His call (3:5).

We cannot follow God if we do not understand that His ways are unique from our own. He is not like us, and His requirements suit His unique being:

Exodus 3:5 Then He said, "Do not come near here; remove your sandals from your feet, for the place on which you are standing is holy ground."

Faith is about seeing God and His world as He says it truly is. It is fundamentally about trusting in His character and following Him into the uncertain future, certain of His character alone. He is distinct from us, and we dare not try to reduce Him to our level. He is wholly above us, and He alone deserves the highest place.

Seventh, recognizing God's identity is essential to following Him wholly (3:6).

God wants you to know **HIM** before you know what He wants you to do! The prize is His companionship in a shared life:

Exodus 3:6 He said also, "I am the God of your father, the God of Abraham, the God of Isaac, and the God of Jacob." Then Moses hid his face, for he was afraid to look at God.

The God of Abraham is not "one of the paths" to eternity, or to the Promised Land. He **alone** is the author of life. He alone is the Creator of all things. He is the Past, and He holds the future firmly.

Colossians 1:15 reminds us: *He is the image of the invisible God, the firstborn of all creation. 16 For by Him all things were created, both in the heavens and on Earth, visible and invisible, whether thrones or dominions or rulers or authorities—all things have been created through Him and for Him. 17 He is before all things, and in Him all things hold together.*

Let me illustrate. One morning during Gladys Aylward's harrowing journey out of war-torn Yang Chen during the Communist take-over, she was faced with no apparent hope of reaching safety. A 13-year old girl tried to comfort her by saying, "Don't forget what you told us about Moses in the wilderness," to which Gladys Aylward replied, "Yes, my dear, but I am not Moses." The young girl replied, "Yes, but God is still God." Isn't that a stunning reminder?

Eighth, listening to God's Word is the key to understanding His intent in the plan (3:7).

God shows His character and His care through His Word. When we take the time to "listen" to what God said, we see what He is like in profound ways:

Exodus 3:7 The LORD said, "I have surely seen the affliction of My people who are in Egypt, and have given heed to their cry because of their taskmasters, for I am aware of their sufferings."

The aloof God proclaimed by those who only know Him in theory has little to do with your real call. Daniel was called to follow God in obedience all the way to the lion's den. God was aware, but He had a plan for Daniel. We love the story because the end is great, but it could just as easily have been a different end. We must understand that God sees when we hurt, hears when we cry, and knows when we are confused – even about Him! Staying close to His words will keep us warm in a cold world. We won't always know where He is going, but we will feel the warmth of His heart.

Ninth, the plan is God's – because He alone knows what He desires to accomplish.

We have the joy of being used by Him for but a brief few moments! We must cherish each one:

Exodus 3:8 So I have come down to deliver them from the power of the Egyptians, and to bring them up from that land to a good and spacious land, to a land flowing with milk and honey, to the place of the Canaanite and the Hittite and the Amorite and the Perizzite and the Hivite and the Jebusite. 9 Now, behold, the cry of the sons of Israel has come to Me;

furthermore, I have seen the oppression with which the Egyptians are oppressing them.

If everything else seems uncertain, of this be clear – **God created you for a purpose**, and He has a plan for your life. You have been served notice. You are called. If you never heard it before, you are hearing it now. You are on a divine mission. God has set you on a path – and you must follow Him to arrive where He intends your life to go.

Maybe it would help to offer a graphic picture. The cocoon of the Emperor moth is flask-like in shape. To develop into a perfect insect, it must force its way through the neck of the cocoon by hours of intense struggle. Entomologists explain that this pressure to which the moth is subjected is nature's way of forcing a life-giving substance into its wings. Wanting to lessen the seemingly needless trials and struggles of the moth, an observer said, "I'll lesson the pain and struggles of this helpless creature!" With small scissors he snipped the restraining threads to make the moth's emergence painless and effortless. The creature never developed wings. For a brief time before its death, it simply crawled instead of flying through the air on rainbow colored wings! (By the way, the struggles of childbirth – that is, the child squeezing through the birth canal are also a God-designed way of forcing liquid out of the newborn's lungs.) Sorrow, suffering, trials, and tribulations are wisely designed to grow us into Christlikeness. The refining and developing processes are oftentimes slow, but through grace, we emerge triumphant. Because it is painful, does not mean it is bad – it may be exactly what we need.

Tenth, God gets to tell me my position, priorities and my purpose.

Every other idea I have of happiness must be subject to His expressed will:

Exodus 3:10 Therefore, come now, and I will send you to Pharaoh, so that you may bring My people, the sons of Israel, out of Egypt.

I was created to reflect His image, and fulfill His purpose. It is a God-sized challenge, and self- sufficiency is no longer an option. His strength is required for my success in the mission – I cannot do it apart from that. Know this: We must not be surprised that what God asked of us yesterday is insufficient to journey with Him today. Each day is new, and each turn in the road will require new choices to follow Him.

This story made me smile, because it helps us see God at work in and through us: It was Sunday morning and Harry was off. He pulled out of his driveway in his 2-seater convertible with the roof closed because of typical Melbourne driving rain, and headed for church. But as he turned into the main road he saw ahead of him three bedraggled figures huddled under a single umbrella at the next bus stop. One was old Mrs. Fletcher. She still insisted on getting to church by herself, despite her arthritis, which was always worse in wet weather. There was Dr. Jones, the local GP. A year earlier Dr. Jones had diagnosed a rare and dangerous disease that Harry had contracted on an overseas holiday, so Harry virtually owed him his life. And the third person was Judith. Harry had had a crush on Judith for the past 6 months since she joined their church but had never had the courage or the opportunity to ask her out. Harry had about 3 seconds to decide what to do. There was only one spare seat. Who should he offer a lift to? But 3 seconds was enough. He pulled to a halt, jumped out, passed the keys to Dr. Jones, helped Mrs. Fletcher into the passenger seat, then modestly waved them "good-bye" as he huddled close to Judith under the umbrella. It is nice to know that God's sovereignty and our action so often go hand in hand. (That makes me smile).

Do you want God to win in the tug of war on your heart? Remember that God's call is not mystical. **He has set the pattern for how He calls men and women to service for Him** – but we must understand the pattern and identify His call in our lives.

Grasping God's Purpose: Lessons in Exodus

Lesson Four: Exodus 3:10-4:18 "Your identification, please!"

To get on flights, our need for clear and certain identification has dramatically increased. You can't go back to the gate without a security check on your gate pass. You can't get a gate pass without proper identification. We live in a time when the link between identification and security makes sense to virtually everyone who has not lived under a rock for the last decade. In dangerous times like these, it is particularly important that people are made to prove who they are.

Believers also have a need to carry identity marks with us. We need to know WHO we are, and WHOSE we are. We are the loved, sought-after and redeemed servants of the Great King. These words are not new to you. Much has been said and written about our IDENTITY in Christ – but that is NOT the subject of our study today. In this lesson, we want to look at something that has been very often neglected.

Too little has been exposed about another identity that is the key to really walking with God --- understanding His identity. The *"fear of the Lord is the beginning of knowledge" (Proverbs 1:7).* That knowledge is about us, our world, and our destiny. It is all the knowledge worth knowing – and it is rooted in knowing Who the King truly is in character.

When a believer doesn't really recognize that God has the ultimate power to change a heart even though yielded to Him, he or she is limited to righteousness they can self-produce.

That will always be accompanied by a gnawing sense that real power is missing, because real presence is lacking. Flesh displaces Spirit, and the work of God becomes the works of a man or woman.

Key Principle: A believer who walks with God in power is a believer who has found and confounded a crucial LIE of the enemy – success of God's mission in us depends on our abilities.

Our success in doing God's desires is not bounded by our abilities, but by our understanding of and submission to God's power…

This lesson is about a time **before** Moses was a great leader. It was his classroom time in the Midianite desert seminary class. The teacher was the Creator of man. The lesson was about Moses' four flawed views that pushed him to four flawed conclusions. Let's peek from behind the rocks and listen in to the conversation between the Most High and the leader in training…Our lesson can be split into three simple components: God's Call (3:10), Moses' Problems (3:11-4:17). and Moses' Submission (4:18).

First, God's Call (3:10):

Exodus 3:10 Therefore, come now, and I will send you to Pharaoh, so that you may bring My people, the sons of Israel, out of Egypt.

Note two things about the call:

- It is based on what God had already shared – hence the word "*therefore.*" We saw in the previous lesson that Moses was not eligible to work for God until Moses recognized the Holiness of God (3:5). In addition, the call was based on the knowledge of the Character of God (3:6-7) based on His history with specific men recorded in His Word.

- The call was certain in its goals but unspecific in process. God didn't detail every part of the plan – just the purpose of the venture.

Second, Moses' Problems: (Exodus 3:11-4:17)

God often encounters objections. Here are the common ones:

- *WHO -- ME*? Looking to my insufficient ability not recognizing His empowering presence (3:11-12). I don't have the stature to pull this off (Ex. 3:11)

Exodus 3:11 But Moses said to God, "Who am I, that I should go to Pharaoh, and that I should bring the sons of Israel out of Egypt?"

Look at the nature of this common objection to following God's will. What is the real issue in Moses' thinking here? The real issue is that Moses somehow has the impression that God is delegating the purpose of the mission and is not willing to supply all that is needed to accomplish the mission.

The idea Moses had is not an unfamiliar one – and that is God has stranded us on a fallen island with a purpose of making changes we cannot pull off. In and of itself it is not untrue – it is just unfinished.

What God calls a man or woman to do will be done by GOD through that man or woman. We don't have to DO it, we have to ALLOW IT to be done through us. What does that mean in practice? It means constant communion with God to allow each small choice to follow His direction.

God's response was: You are looking in the wrong direction! My *Presence* (3:12a) and My *Promise* (3:12b) are what goes with you!

Exodus3:12 And He said, "Certainly I will be with you, and this shall be the sign to you that it is I who have sent you:

when you have brought the people out of Egypt, you shall worship God at this mountain."

God offers nothing but Himself, for there is nothing (and no one) higher for Him to offer.

Ultimately, the ability argument comes down to one LIE we believe – that God isn't big enough to pull off what He says He will do. Christians often swallow that LIE.

- They believe God can save them, but not that He can give them the power to conquer their addictions.
- They believe He can raise the dead, but not that He can soften them to forgive an enemy, or overcome a racial prejudice.
- They believe the Spirit empowers them, but not that they have all they need to live a godly life in Christ Jesus

How's that? Looking at my insufficient understanding not trusting His continuing direction (3:13-22). I lack sufficient long term knowledge to get this job done (3:13).

Exodus 3:13 Then Moses said to God, "Behold, I am going to the sons of Israel, and I will say to them, 'The God of your fathers has sent me to you.' Now they may say to me, 'What is His name?' What shall I say to them?"

God's response was: I will fill you in (3:14-15).

Exodus 3:14 God said to Moses, "I AM WHO I AM," and He said, "Thus you shall say to the sons of Israel, 'I AM has sent me to you.'" 15 God, furthermore, said to Moses, "Thus you shall say to the sons of Israel, 'The LORD, the God of your fathers, the God of Abraham, the God of Isaac, and the God of Jacob, has sent me to you.' This is My name forever, and this is My memorial-name to all generations." 15 God, furthermore, said to Moses, "Thus you shall say to the sons of Israel, 'The LORD, the God of your fathers, the God of Abraham, the God of Isaac, and the God of Jacob, has sent me to you.' This is My name forever, and this is My memorial-name to all generations."

I have a plan (3:16-17).

Exodus 3:16 "Go and gather the elders of Israel together and say to them, 'The LORD, the God of your fathers, the God of Abraham, Isaac and Jacob, has appeared to me, saying, "I am indeed concerned about you and what has been done to you in Egypt. 17 So I said, I will bring you up out of the affliction of Egypt to the land of the Canaanite and the Hittite and the Amorite and the Perizzite and the Hivite and the Jebusite, to a land flowing with milk and honey."'

It will not go without challenges (3:18-20)

Exodus 3:18 "They will pay heed to what you say; and you with the elders of Israel will come to the king of Egypt and you will say to him, 'The LORD, the God of the Hebrews, has met with us. So now, please, let us go a three days' journey into the wilderness, that we may sacrifice to the LORD our God.' 19 But I know that the king of Egypt will not permit you to go, except under compulsion. 20 So I will stretch out My hand and strike Egypt with all My miracles which I shall do in the midst of it; and after that he will let you go."

Yet, I have a long term purpose for these short-term, painful delays (3:21-22)

Exodus 3:21 "I will grant this people favor in the sight of the Egyptians; and it shall be that when you go, you will not go empty-handed. 22 But every woman shall ask of her neighbor and the woman who lives in her house, articles of silver and articles of gold, and clothing; and you will put them on your sons and daughters. Thus you will plunder the Egyptians."

Moses answered God (4:1).

Moses wasn't so sure. Looking at his tiny faith and failing to embrace God's promises… Moses feared the reaction of the people (4:1-9). I don't think they will believe me (4:1)

Exodus 4:1 Then Moses said, "What if they will not believe me or listen to what I say? For they may say, 'The LORD has not appeared to you.'"

Note that God had already given the truth in *3:18: They will pay heed to what you say; and you with the elders of Israel will come to the king of Egypt…*

The issue here was one of first **truly believing what God said** was true, and then so changing his actions to conform to the reality as God said it would be. God knows the truth, and we must believe what He says about it – no matter whether that conforms to our past experience or not.

God answered: I will send you with power (4:2-9).

Exodus 2 The LORD said to him, "What is that in your hand?" And he said, "A staff." 3 Then He said, "Throw it on the ground." So he threw it on the ground, and it became a serpent; and Moses fled from it. 4 But the LORD said to Moses, "Stretch out your hand and grasp it by its tail"—so he stretched out his hand and caught it, and it became a staff in his hand— 5 "that they may believe that the LORD, the God of their fathers, the God of Abraham, the God of Isaac, and the God of Jacob, has appeared to you." 6 The LORD furthermore said to him, "Now put your hand into your bosom." So he put his hand into his bosom, and when he took it out, behold, his hand was leprous like snow. 7 Then He said, "Put your hand into your bosom again." So he put his hand into his bosom again, and when he took it out of his bosom, behold, it was restored like the rest of his flesh. 8 "If they will not believe you or heed the witness of the first sign, they may believe the witness of the last sign. 9 But if they will not believe even these two signs or heed what you say, then you shall take some water from the Nile and pour it on the dry ground; and the water which you take from the Nile will become blood on the dry ground." *(Emphasis R. Smith)*

Note four essential truths here:

First, God has never promised to empower your abilities to meet your plans, but has never failed to supply His own power to His plan. God asks Moses, "What is in your hand?" God empowers what we have, and has never demanded from us submission of what we do not have. We are called to be willing to offer ourselves to God. God selected you based already on ability – or you wouldn't have the call to do the work. Now He is looking for availability. God knows that what He called you to do can only be successfully done WITH YOU in daily lock step WITH HIM. That isn't unusual – it is the plan.

Second, God calls you to follow His Word, even when it is counterintuitive and contradistinctive to your past experience. I don't know how you pick up a snake, but I am sure picking it up by the tail was not a natural experience!

Third, God needs to remind us continually that our flesh is weak, temporary and unstable. We think we are dependable, but we can defect in heart at any moment and become utterly useless, defective and DEFILED. Leprosy of the hand shouted this lesson to Moses

.

Fourth, God alone can restore what is broken because of the human rebellion. We walk in the power of the Redeemer, with knowledge that redemption is not complete yet. When God restored the hand of Moses, the man got the message.

The problem was that Moses was looking at his insufficient resources not resting in God's sufficiency (4:1-10-18). He didn't have the inner abilities to do this work – but that wasn't what God asked him to bring with him (4:10).

Exodus 4:10 Then Moses said to the LORD, "Please, Lord, I have never been eloquent, neither recently nor in time past, nor since You have spoken to Your servant; for I am slow of speech and slow of tongue."

God answered: I happen to know your problems quite well (4:11-12).

Exodus 4:11 The LORD said to him, "Who has made man's mouth? Or who makes him mute or deaf, or seeing or blind? Is it not I, the LORD? 12 "Now then go, and I, even I, will be with your mouth, and teach you what you are to say."

Our inadequacies are not a problem for our Creator - He made us the way we are. Our issue is only one – will we make ourselves available to God's use? If not, no amount of ability will make our lives go forward. Athletes and celebrities – talented all – have proven over and over that ability is not the singular key to success. Moses was also wrongly looking at "accommodation with God's plan" and not "surrendering to God's sovereignty" and following the plan exactly as given (4:13). In essence he told God: "I like the plan, but would prefer *not* to participate at that level" (4:13).

Exodus 4:13 But he said, "Please, Lord, now send the message by whomever You will."

Here lies the great real problem in our hearts – we are making excuses because we don't want to do what God says. We want it to get done, to be sure, but we don't want to be the ones inconvenienced to do it.

I love this illustration from *Moody Monthly* a few years ago about why people don't want to go to church, but find it easier to make excuses. The author intelligently used the same excuses he heard about church on quitting being a sport's fan. Listen to how stupid the excuses sound:

"Every time I went they asked for money. The people with whom I had to sit didn't seem very friendly. The seats were too hard and uncomfortable. The coach never came to see me. The referee made a decision with which I could not agree. I was sitting with some hypocrites – they only came to see what others were wearing. Some games went into overtime, and I was late getting home. The band played numbers that I had never heard before. The games were scheduled when I want to do other things. My parents took me to too many games when I was growing up. Since I read a book on sports, I feel that I know more than the coaches anyhow. I don't want to take my children, because I want them to choose for themselves what sport they like best." (quoted by Charles Swindoll, *The Tale of the Tardy Oxcart and 1,501 Other Stories,* Nashville: Word, 1998. p. 189).

Now it doesn't skip my notice that those who are engaged in this lesson probably aren't offering excuses about going to church, but we do offer excuses to God about holding the reins of our lives in other ways. Just remember, God's anger was a word that judgment comes to the one who won't give up their excuses. Remember this: Dr. B. J. Miller once said, "It is a great deal easier to do that which God gives us to do, no matter how hard it is, than to face the responsibilities of not doing it". (MBI's *Today In The Word*, November, 1989, p.11)

When we truly believe that, we act in God's desires.

God answered: Let me send another with you (4:14-17).

Exodus 4:14 Then the anger of the LORD burned against Moses, and He said, "Is there not your brother Aaron the Levite? I know that he speaks fluently. And moreover, behold, he is coming out to meet you; when he sees you, he will be glad in his heart. 15 You are to speak to him and put the words in his mouth; and I, even I, will be with your mouth and his mouth, and I will teach you what you are to do. 16 Moreover, he shall speak for you to the people; and he will be as a mouth for you and you will be as God to him. 17 You shall take in your hand this staff, with which you shall perform the signs..."

Remember, Aaron became a problem at a number of key points in Moses' journey!

God accommodated Moses, but the compromise was not God's best in Moses' life. Aaron got the children of Israel into serious trouble with God at the mountain! **Following God's true desire is always better than sliding through the task in His permissive and patient will!**

Sometimes our excuses pile up and get in the way of doing something for God. I read a humorous story about some GI's on furlough that I think illustrates this: "The commanding officer was furious when nine GIs who had been out on passes failed to show up for morning roll call. Not until 7 p.m. did the first man straggle in. "I'm sorry, sir," the soldier explained, "but I had a date and lost track of time, and I missed the bus back. Being determined to get in on time, I hired a cab. Halfway here, the cab broke down. I went to a farmhouse and persuaded the farmer to sell me a horse. I was riding to camp when the animal fell over dead. I walked the last ten miles, and just got here." Though skeptical, the Colonel let the young man off with a reprimand. However, after him, seven other stragglers in a row came in with the same story -had a date, missed the bus, hired a cab, bought a horse, etc. By the time the ninth man reported in, the colonel had grown weary of it. "Okay," he growled, "now what happened to you?" "Sir, I had this date and missed the bus back, so I hired a cab." "Wait!" the colonel screeched at him. "Don't tell me the cab broke down." "No, sir," replied the soldier. "The cab didn't break down. It was just that there were so many dead horses in the road, we had trouble getting through." Excuses! (Contributed by John F. King, *speaking illustrator*)

Third, Moses' Submission (4:18)

Exodus 4:18 Then Moses departed and returned to Jethro his father-in-law and said to him, "Please, let me go, that I may return to my brethren who are in Egypt, and see if they are still alive." And Jethro said to Moses, "Go in peace."

In the Fall, man was blinded to God's power and promises. He was made ignorant of the Holy One in all His glory. That ignorance left us drawing the conclusion that God must be like us - the potter was like the clay. We grew arrogant and thought we could conclude that He would only do what WE would do. He was subject to our limited thinking. His plans must be fit into OUR boxes. Even as believers, the old man still haunts us because our identity in Christ is only PART of the equation – the other part is the poorly constructed IDENTITY of GOD. **Our ability to do the work of Christ is not constrained by our abilities so much as by our conception of God.**

The bottom line is that we say, "I can't" – when what we really mean is, "I won't!" Let's face the facts …we disobey because we choose to… not because we have to. Taking responsibility for that, and walking in intimacy and surrender, will make my life say what God created it to say.

Grasping God's Purpose: Lessons in Exodus

Lesson Five: Exodus 4:14-3 "Heeding the Call"

Running away from your call is not safe! Did you get a call on your cell phone this week, see the name of the person calling, and decide not to take the call? Don't roll your eyes; it happens on every street in our city. Let's be positive…Sometimes the problem is **timing**: You want to take the call but the caller has caught you in the check-out line at the grocery store, or in the middle of a very loud restaurant – and you know you won't be able to hear. Maybe they will even call you while you are in church this week! Calls often come at the most inconvenient times!

Sometimes it isn't the timing so much as the **demand**. You know what the caller wants! Because you have not fulfilled some obligation, or attended a meeting, or prepared your part of some project, or met some expectation - you know what is coming – and you'd like to avoid it for now. Still other times, it isn't the demand, it is the **personality**: You just aren't ready to deal with that particular person in the mood you are in. Do you have people that drain out your enthusiasm as quickly as pulling a plug in the bathtub?

Just because we *get* a call, doesn't mean we are going to be willing to *take* the call. We have learned how to avoid hearing and responding to what we don't choose to allow in our lives. We have so honed that ability that it has become a lethal option – because we think we can even put the Creator on HOLD… but we must not.

Key Principle: God's people must be prepared to hear God's call, and move at His direction. To do so, we must know how to appropriately respond.

In our study in Exodus, we have wrestled with great questions. We saw the people of Israel struggle as they asked, "Why does God allow punishing times of trouble in our lives?" We sat behind the rock at Mt. Horeb and watched Moses in his conversation with God as he asked, "Who can God really use?" We probed the question: "What is God's call?" "How do I know what God wants me to do with the life He has given me?"

Today we are still hiding behind that rock on the Holy Mountain. We are listening to God talk with Moses, but God's voice is agitated. In fact, He is downright ticked off. Following Moses' attempt to ignore the call of God, we can see how God used him in spite of himself. That presses on us yet another question:

"What do I do when I get a call from God?"

First, let's look at this short story from the Word:

Exodus 4:14 Then the anger of the LORD burned against Moses, and He said, "Is there not your brother Aaron the Levite? I know that he speaks fluently. And moreover, behold, he is coming out to meet you; when he sees you, he will be glad in his heart. 15 You are to speak to him and put the words in his mouth; and I, even I, will be with your mouth and his mouth, and I will teach you what you are to do. 16 Moreover, he shall speak for you to the people; and he will be as a mouth for you and you will be as God to him. 17 You shall take in your hand this staff, with which you shall perform the signs." 18 Then Moses departed and returned to Jethro his father-in-law and said to him, "Please, let me go, that I may return to my brethren who are in Egypt, and see if they are still alive." And Jethro said to Moses, "Go in peace." 19 Now the LORD said to Moses in Midian, "Go back to Egypt, for all the men who were seeking your life are dead." 20 So Moses took his wife and his sons and mounted them on a donkey, and returned to the land of Egypt. Moses also took the staff of God in his hand. 21 The LORD said to Moses, "When you go back to Egypt see that you perform before Pharaoh all the wonders which I have put in your power; but I will harden his heart so that he will not let the people go. 22 Then you shall say to Pharaoh, 'Thus says the LORD, "Israel is My son, My firstborn.' 23 So I said to you, 'Let My son go that he may serve Me'; but you have refused to let him go. Behold, I will kill your son, your firstborn.'" 24 Now it came about at the lodging place on the way that the LORD met him and sought to put him to death. 25 Then Zipporah took a flint and cut off her son's foreskin and threw it at Moses' feet, and she said, "You are indeed a bridegroom of blood to me." 26 So He let him alone. At that time she said, "You are a bridegroom of blood"—because of the circumcision. 27 Now the LORD said to Aaron, "Go to meet Moses in the wilderness." So he went and met him at the mountain of God and kissed him. 28 Moses told Aaron all the words of the LORD with which He had sent him, and all the signs that He had commanded him to do. 29 Then Moses and Aaron went and assembled all the elders of the sons of Israel; 30 and Aaron spoke all the words which the LORD had spoken to Moses. He then performed the signs in the sight of the people. 31 So the people believed; and when they heard that the LORD was concerned about the sons of Israel and that He had seen their affliction, then they bowed low and worshiped. (Emphasis mine)

Before we get deeply into the story, note that Moses has been in trouble twice here. First, God was really ticked at him. Later, God's displeasure became even worse – now his wife was mad at him. Every man studying this passage can sympathize. Poor Mo, things aren't going well for a while! The problem wasn't God's call – it was Moses' reaction to God's call on his life… and perhaps someone here can feel this inside in a unique way. Remember this if you forget everything else in this lesson…

Running from God's call in your life is not safe.

When God calls, I must respond. Fortunately He gave me eight guidelines to follow so I can have confidence in my response – If I do respond as He said:

First, I should listen to His call carefully (4:14-17).

Quit fussing about my abilities and limitations and listen to Him, believing He can accomplish His will through me!

Exodus 4:14 Then the anger of the LORD burned against Moses, and He said, "Is there not your brother Aaron the Levite? I know that he speaks fluently. And moreover, behold, he is coming out to meet you; when he sees you, he will be glad in his heart. 15 You are to speak to him and put the words in his mouth; and I, even I, will be with your mouth and his mouth, and I will teach you what you are to do. 16 Moreover, he shall speak for you to the people; and he will be as a mouth for you and you will be as God to him. 17 You shall take in your hand this staff, with which you shall perform the signs."

Look closely from behind our rock and see Moses' hand. What is in it? It looks like a stick - a dead piece of old tree. A has been of botany. It could not, of itself, bring life. It was just something dead to lean on, to balance himself – or to rescue sheep from a crevasse. Moses had no ideaIDEA what important plans God had for the stick in his hand!

This rod was just like him - nothing special of itself apart from the power of God! God took and empowered what Moses had.

One author wrote, "God never asks what we don't have to give. Most of us have insufficient resources – emotional, physical, financial, etc. Most of us don't have sufficient knowledge or education to accomplish the call to reach, well – anyone. I begin to hear the words of Paul: "Not many wise, not many mighty…" (You get the idea). Let's just say that in the world's ranking, Donald Trump is more than likely not to give up his restaurant seat when we come to the door. We just aren't that important. Yet, to God's call we are essential. We are the one God is calling and God never directs our attention to what we don't have, but to what we do have even though it seems small. God gave us everything we needed to do the job! Even though what we have seems small, weak, and insignificant.

God doesn't often choose the powerful on purpose - because God designed His work through us in a way that we must be connected to Him to work His plan. In every call, the difference is the power of God. It is not our ability, our knowledge, our talent, or the size of our gifts or the beauty of our gift that matters. All that matters is: How much of what you have do you yield for God to empower – or, how much "God is in your stick?" Your stick represents surrender to God. Alone it is dead. When God gets in it, it's enough! When God gets in it, it will surprise you – don't forget that Moses fled from before his rod when it turned into a serpent.

The empowering is the supernatural power of God operating through the natural to produce results that are humanly impossible. We need to ask God to get in our staff. That is to say the great need of the hour is God in our song, God in our preaching, God in our marriage, God in our parenting, God in our business, God in our gift, God in our talent. When God gets in a thing, it is not the same. When God gets in a thing it can scare some people - just like Moses who had never seen his rod do anything like that before.

- God got in a **rock** and caused a river to flow out of it that quenched the thirst of the nation of Israelites.
- God got in a **donkey** and caused it to speak and rebuke a rebellious prophet.
- God got in an **axe** head of iron and caused it to swim up to the top of the water so the prophet could reach out his hand and take hold of it.
- God got in a little **pot of oil** and caused it to multiply till it met every need and provided an abundant overflow.

Moses' rod symbolizes something that is weak; it has no life or energy of its own. It could only do what the natural man's power enabled it to do - until the power of God got in it.

That isn't the only lesson. There is another truth from the stick:

When God wants to give us something new, something greater, we have to be willing to let go of the control of what we have.

We have to trust God with our stick. Before God fulfilled his promise to Abraham that all the nations of the Earth would be blessed in his seed, He asked for his seed back – the son of Abraham became the son of God. In this story, the rod of Moses became *the rod of God*. In that way, the rod became the symbol of God's authority and God's power - an instrument by which God's Word and will were demonstrated. When Moses stretched out the rod, it was a type of speaking the Word out of a believing heart.

One of the greatest problems we have as believers is we have a tendency to underestimate what we have. Another is the tendency to think the stick is still ours. Look what God did with a surrendered stick! So I must ask.... "What is in *your* hands?" (Adapted from *sermon central illustrations*, original author unknown)

Second, I should show respect to those in authority over my life (4:18).

Don't just go running off and blame God for not meeting my obligations!

Exodus 4:18 Then Moses departed and returned to Jethro his father-in-law and said to him, "Please, let me go, that I may return to my brethren who are in Egypt, and see if they are still alive." And Jethro said to Moses, "Go in peace."

When we get into the "God called me" mode, we dare not forget the people God made me responsible for. We don't shed all our prior agreements and responsibilities to run off – that isn't God's way. Moses' example is just one of many. God works through responsible people who meet their word. If permission is delayed, then God is at work. Did not God say this very thing in regard to Pharaoh not letting the people leave? It was in His plan for His purpose – to get the wealth of the Egyptians into the hands of the Israelite slaves before they go home!

Delays are less significant than disrespect. God can work through the delays, but chafes against using those disrespectful to His commands. **The truth is that a self-willed soldier is unpredictable – and often useless in the time of battle.** God most often works through those who are respectful, obedient and patient to accomplish God's call.

Third, I should trust that God has prepared the way!

If God is calling, He will provide the way (4:19). Moses recalled:

Exodus 4:19 Now the LORD said to Moses in Midian, "Go back to Egypt, for all the men who were seeking your life are dead."

Prudence is a God thing – but trust is also. Moses had a perfectly acceptable check in his heart about going back – it was called a "wanted poster." God removed the check by telling him that although the issues were still fresh in HIS LIFE, the nation had moved on – and he was no longer in danger

.
Those behind the bounty on his head were gone, and the post office was now filled with new faces to line the walls on wanted posters. At 80, they assumed his killing spree was limited to one rash act.

We have said it often: "Where God guides, God provides." Sometimes it is found in God filling the need for provision. Just as often it is God removing the obstacles.

Fourth, I should step out and accept the help that God has given me for the journey! (4:20)

God provides help, but often we resist it, or don't see it, because it is so familiar to us, and we think God should send something more dramatic:

Exodus 4: 20 So Moses took his wife and his sons and mounted them on a donkey, and returned to the land of Egypt. Moses also took the staff of God in his hand.

"Flash floods were sweeping the area around the rivers in our country's interior. Volunteers risked their lives to rescue victims stranded in the deluge. One old man was in his front yard, up to his knees in the rising waters when a rowboat came. "Hop in, we'll save you!" "No thanks, the Lord will provide." A short while later, a motor boat was sent to save him. By this time the swirling waters were over his waist, but again he declined: "No thanks, the Lord will provide." Soon the water was up to his chin, so a helicopter was dispatched at the last minute. 'Climb aboard, this is your last chance!" "Thanks anyway, but I don't need you, the Lord will provide.' "Before the hour ended, the old man perished and found himself banging on the Pearly Gates. He bitterly complained to St. Peter, 'I prayed and I prayed for you to help me, so why did you let me drown?' St. Peter looked at him, shook his head, and explained: 'Good grief, we sent you two boats and a helicopter. What more do you want?'" (*Preaching Illustrations*)

Just like looking at the stick, we have to look at those assigned to us on the journey and know that God put the team together. He is aware of the need to inhabit them – just like He did to the stick! He is able, and we need to trust that

Fifth, I should rehearse often the revelation of God in my life (4:21-23).

My encouragement is drawn from recognizing surrendered obedience to His call – not through the apparent "success of the mission."

Exodus 4:21 The LORD said to Moses, "When you go back to Egypt see that you perform before Pharaoh all the wonders which I have put in your power; but I will harden his heart so that he will not let the people go. 22 Then you shall say to Pharaoh, 'Thus says the LORD, "Israel is My son, My firstborn. 23 So I said to you, 'Let My son go that he may serve Me'; but you have refused to let him go. Behold, I will kill your son, your firstborn."'"

If I don't continually remind myself of God's call, I will become discouraged with the experience of following God. It doesn't matter the size of the project, the problem will be the same. I will look at the people and problems around me and forget that NONE OF THEM are an obstacle to me completing what God truly wants – the transformation of my mind and the surrender of my heart. **God doesn't need me to do anything – He wants me to enjoy the cooperative experience of completing His empowered task**

Sixth, I should fully obey what God has told me (4:24-26).

My new call doesn't cancel my obedience to prior commands. Partial obedience is disobedience, and disobedience is terribly dangerous to us and all those around us!

Exodus 4:24 Now it came about at the lodging place on the way that the LORD met him and sought to put him to death. 25 Then Zipporah took a flint and cut off her son's foreskin and threw it at Moses' feet, and she said, "You are indeed a bridegroom of blood to me." 26 So He let him alone. At that time she said, "You are a bridegroom of blood"—because of the circumcision.

I like the pastor that wrote: “Thank God for a strong wife! At a family gathering, a woman and her cousin were being teased by their husbands about how they always get their way. ‘Honey,’ the cousin said to her husband, ‘when I get my way, that’s a compromise.’ ‘What is it when I get my way?’ he was quick to ask. She replied, ‘That’s a miracle!’"

While there Moses has two sons by his wife Zipporah: **Gershom** (which means "**Alien**") and **Eliezer** (meaning "**God is my helper**"). Gershom appears to have been the eldest and was likely born while Moses was feeling alienated from his people and his home in Egypt.

This obscure story from Moses’ life can be confusing unless we consider some of the facts involved: In Genesis 17:9-14 we are reminded that God required Abraham to circumcise his family as a sign of the covenant:

Genesis 17:9-14 This is my covenant with you and your descendants after you, the covenant you are to keep: Every male among you shall be circumcised. You are to undergo circumcision, and it will be the sign of the covenant between Me and you. For the generations to come every male among you who is eight days old must be circumcised, including those born in your household or bought with money from a foreigner-- those who are not your offspring (Gen 17:10-12).

Seventh, I should accept from God the team of those I will serve with (4:27-30a).

We can always find reasons why they aren’t good enough – but that isn’t our call!

Exodus 4:27 Now the LORD said to Aaron, “Go to meet Moses in the wilderness.” So he went and met him at the mountain of God and kissed him. 28 Moses told Aaron all the words of the LORD with which He had sent him, and all the signs that He had commanded him to do. 29 Then Moses and Aaron went and assembled all the elders of the sons of Israel; 30 and Aaron spoke all the words which the LORD had spoken to Moses. ...

What would have been the record of the story if Moses or Aaron spent their first year together deciding if the other truly was called of God to do the work? What would have been accomplished while they were litmus testing each other? Pretty much nothing. I am not saying that we don't need to understand the rest of the team – but it must be done through eyes of appreciation for what God has given us to work with!

Eighth, I should use the empowering of God, and not just my limited abilities! (4:30b-31).

My performance is less significant when it is a display of ability, and far greater when it shows His hand in my life:

Exodus 4:30b: He then performed the signs in the sight of the people. 31 So the people believed; and when they heard that the LORD was concerned about the sons of Israel and that He had seen their affliction, then they bowed low and worshiped

This was written some years ago, and is dated – but it expresses well the sentiment:

IT DEPENDS WHOSE HANDS IT'S IN

A basketball in my hands is worth about $19. A basketball in Michael Jordan's hands is worth about $33 million. It depends whose hands it's in.

A baseball in my hands is worth about $6. A baseball in Mark McGuire's hands is worth $19 million. It depends whose hands it's in.

A tennis racket is useless in my hands. A tennis racket in Pete Sampras' hands is a Wimbledon Championship. It depends whose hands it's in.

A rod in my hands will keep away a wild animal. A rod in Moses' hands will part the mighty sea. It depends whose hands it's in.

A sling shot in my hands is a kid's toy. A sling shot in David's hand is a mighty weapon. It depends whose hands it's in.

Two fish and five loaves of bread in my hands are a couple of fish sandwiches. Two fish and five loaves of bread in Jesus' hands will feed thousands. It depends whose hands they're in.

Nails in my hands might produce a birdhouse. Nails in Jesus Christ's hands will produce salvation for the entire world. It depends Whose hands they're in.

As you see, now it depends Whose hands it's in. So put your concerns, your worries, your fears, your hopes, your dreams, your families and your relationships in God's hands because
It depends Whose hands they're in. (*Author Unknown*)

God's people must be prepared to hear God's call, and move at His direction. to do so, we must know how to respond.

Grasping God's Purpose: Lessons in Exodus

Lesson Six: Exodus 4:27-5:23 "The Key to Success"

What is the definition of success? Is that a senseless question? Think about it… is it really?

People are spending away their lives desperately seeking this illusive dream – **do we even know what success is** in life? The question is simple enough, but the answer seems so personalized and difficult to grasp for many. For most of us, success is measured by our sense of happiness. If wealth were success – then the richest people would be the happiest. If physical condition was the measure, then body-builders would be happier than the rest of us. If personal freedom was the measure, then the unattached homeless man or woman would be the happiest and thereby most successful among us.

A popular website claims: "Achieving personal success does not have to be difficult. Success is not an impossible dream. You can become successful in life. The techniques and technologies presented … will show you how to achieve the success you have always wanted, but first you need to know what success means to you, not some general definition of success. …Developing a strong vision of what you will look like when you are truly successful will help you step into that person in your imagination's shoes."
(http://www.squidoo.com/personal_success)

This isn't a self-help seminar put together by a publishing marketer. **Our measure for all things in life** is found by looking carefully at the record of our Creator's manual that is designed to give us what we need to be complete in Him. We look unapologetically at the Word and find the definition for success – but it is not the one the world is familiar with. In the Word we consistently find a single key to success. Even more surprisingly, it is not subjectively measured, as psychologists suggest in our day. It is objective and it is singular - and failure to recognize that truth will open you to a world of wrong turns and false directions. What is success according to God's Word?

Key Principle: To a believer, success is whole hearted obedience to the Word of God – regardless of any external outcomes.

That is a bit hard to swallow. I want to obey and get blessed. I want to obey and be fulfilled. I want, in short, any obedience to turn to blessing that benefits me. The problem is that isn't what I was created for. The whole of life is not to please ME, but to exalt HIM. Let's look more closely, because something as important as my life's success deserves a close look:

The Stage of Failure: (4:27-5:1)

Exodus 4:27 Now the LORD said to Aaron, "Go to meet Moses in the wilderness." So he went and met him at the mountain of God and kissed him. 28 Moses told Aaron all the words of the LORD with which He had sent him, and all the signs that He had commanded him to do. 29 Then Moses and Aaron went and assembled all the elders of the sons of Israel; 30 and Aaron spoke all the words which the LORD had spoken to Moses. He then performed the signs in the sight of the people. 31 So the people believed; and when they heard that the LORD was concerned about the sons of Israel and that He had seen their affliction, then they bowed low and worshiped. 5:1 And afterward Moses and Aaron came and said to Pharaoh, "Thus says the LORD, the God of Israel, 'Let My people go that they may celebrate a feast to Me in the wilderness.'"

In the first few verses of our study, it is clear that Moses seemed easily set up for the disappointment of his encounter with Pharaoh. Like so many instances in life, this seeming failure came on the back of some great successes!

Four "problems" set the stage for failure:

Problem One: Emotional Support:

His long lost brother came back into his life! (4:27)

Moses was feeling good and was relieved by a dear one comforting him. That isn't wrong, but it put a slave on the man instead of helping him to really feel the heat of the anger of God as he tested the Lord in his call. God was upset with Moses' resistance, and then by his disobedience – but Moses was feeling great because his brother was back in his life. Sometimes emotional support is a GOOD THING. However, seeking counsel instead of getting right with God is avoidance. Counselor's offices are filled with people who resist honest prayer and seeking God, and replace that hunger with emotional support systems built in this world.

Problem Two: Affirmation of the crowd: People readily accepted his message (4:31a).

The need that is met by public applause is as deceptive as emotional support that avoids cleansing by God and seeking intimacy with God. Men and women of God must resist getting caught up in the popularity of the moment. We all hunger to be loved and appreciated, but we cannot substitute the inner need to have an intimate and affirming relationship with God for the applause of people who can see only our outer man. We can be lauded by men and failing before God. Conversely, we can be hated by the crowd but hearing in the breeze of the Spirit the subtle clapping of the hands of Heaven. There is nothing wrong with enjoying warm appreciation of others, but we must not come to see that as an indicator of real success – it is often inaccurate.

Problem Three: Camp exhilaration: He joined the crowd as his people worshipped (4:31b).

The people were excited and moved. Moses saw their response and no doubt joined them. It was an infectious drawing in of emotional and spiritual response. How could that be anything but good? The problem is not that their excitement was not good, but rather that it was entirely unreliable as a gauge of whether God was moving in the room. People can come forward by the droves. They can weep and cry. They can publicly display a true desire to change in the midst of the host around them. That, in and of itself, is not a measure of any real work of God. Without a true change of the resistance within to surrender to God – it is merely an emotional exercise. The exercise may help set up surrender, but it is not synonymous with surrender. If you believe this, introspection of full surrender must precede real success. When the emotions of the crowd are whipped up, reality can be harder to detect!

Problem Four: Exhilaration of obedience: He stood before Pharaoh and spoke for God (5:1).

Think carefully about how Moses felt standing before Pharaoh before there was any reply by the national leader. Mo had immediate success at his back, his brother at his side and an exciting and emotionally affirming meeting still ringing in his ears. Now he was standing in Pharaoh's court, stick of God in hand, and blasting out the message the God of Creation had given him.

What Moses needed was the perspective: Things are neither as GOOD nor as BAD as they appear right now. We must not make our decisions based on the "lucky streak" we feel we are having!

Moses was successful, only to the extent that He was doing what God told him to do – the way God told him to do it. It was fun and fulfilling, but that wasn't the point –obedience was! When we forget that truth, we set ourselves up for what happened to Moses a moment later…

The Sound of Failure: (5:2-5)

Scripture offers this insight into failure:

Exodus 5:2 But Pharaoh said, "Who is the LORD that I should obey His voice to let Israel go? I do not know the LORD, and besides, I will not let Israel go." 3 Then they said, "The God of the Hebrews has met with us. Please, let us go a three days journey into the wilderness that we may sacrifice to the LORD our God, otherwise He will fall upon us with pestilence or with the sword." 4 But the king of Egypt said to them, "Moses and Aaron, why do you draw the people away from their work? Get back to your labors!" 5 Again Pharaoh said, "Look, the people of the land are now many, and you would have them cease from their labors!"

Can you hear it - the sound of breaking glass, and a shattered dream? It is the sound of 5:2!

By Moses' reaction, it appears that Pharaoh's response was not what Moses thought would happen (as evidenced by his reaction in 5:22) even though, if he had listened closely, it was exactly what God had promised (3:19-20). Nevertheless, the rejection came painfully. Let's look more closely at two kinds of rejection found in this passage:

- There was "off the radar" rejection: Some rejection is based on the fact that the other person has no appreciation of your values, or your needs (5:2-3). I think it is fair to say that Pharaoh had no problem denying Israel the opportunity to worship a God he thought nothing of. This was not one of the gods of Egypt, and this God was not on his radar screen! The natural reaction to this kind of rejection is to clarify. (5:3).

- Next, we see "motivation" rejection: Some rejection is based on the other person believing we have a different set of motives than we truly do (5:4-5). Pharaoh was concerned that the people with no work would plan mischief, and they were already great in number. He saw no God behind this action, just a former prince of Egypt

Rejection of God's desire in the life of another is not necessarily the failure of God's messenger.

We are tempted to see the rejection of Pharaoh as the moment of failure – but it is NOT! The sound of failure - real failure - was NOT that Pharaoh said no. At the same time, there WAS a failure in the passage on Moses part – the moment he failed to heed what God said.

People, take note! We cannot measure our personal success or failure by how anyone responds to God's message – even if we are the vessel of delivery for the message. If people come to Christ because of your witness, it doesn't mean you are "successful." Conversely, if they reject God but you are obedient to His call, and offer His message His way – success has NOT eluded you.

Remember Gods call to *Jeremiah in 7:27? "You shall speak all these words to them, but they will not listen to you; and you shall call to them, but they will not answer you. 28 You shall say to them, 'This is the nation that did not obey the voice of the LORD their God or accept correction; truth has perished and has been cut off from their mouth. 29 Cut off your hair and cast it away, and take up a lamentation on the bare heights; for the LORD has rejected and forsaken the generation of His wrath.' 30 For the sons of Judah have done that which is evil in My sight," declares the LORD, "they have set their detestable things in the house which is called by My name, to defile it."*

That doesn't give us license to become passive when God commands action. That should not reinforce any laziness on our part. It does, however, remove the burden that comes when we measure our worth by their response, instead of measuring our success by our surrender to Him.

Moses should have, and could have taken refuge in God's call and not Pharaoh's response.

The Surrender to Failure: (5:6-21)

Exodus 5:6 So the same day Pharaoh commanded the
taskmasters over the people and their foremen, saying, 7
"You are no longer to give the people straw to make brick as
previously; let them go and gather straw for themselves. 8
But the quota of bricks which they were making previously,
you shall impose on them; you are not to reduce any of it.
Because they are lazy, therefore they cry out, 'Let us go and
sacrifice to our God.' 9 Let the labor be heavier on the men,
and let them work at it so that they will pay no attention to
false words." 10 So the taskmasters of the people and their
foremen went out and spoke to the people, saying, "Thus
says Pharaoh, 'I am not going to give you any straw. 11 You
go and get straw for yourselves wherever you can find it, but
none of your labor will be reduced.'" 12 So the people
scattered through all the land of Egypt to gather stubble for
straw. 13 The taskmasters pressed them, saying, "Complete
your work quota, your daily amount, just as when you had
straw." 14 Moreover, the foremen of the sons of Israel,
whom Pharaoh's taskmasters had set over them, were beaten
and were asked, "Why have you not completed your required
amount either yesterday or today in making brick as
previously?" 15 Then the foremen of the sons of Israel came
and cried out to Pharaoh, saying, "Why do you deal this way
with your servants? 16 There is no straw given to your

servants, yet they keep saying to us, 'Make bricks!' And behold, your servants are being beaten; but it is the fault of your own people." 17 But he said, "You are lazy, very lazy; therefore you say, 'Let us go and sacrifice to the LORD.' 18 So go now and work; for you will be given no straw, yet you must deliver the quota of bricks." 19 The foremen of the sons of Israel saw that they were in trouble because they were told, "You must not reduce your daily amount of bricks." 20 When they left Pharaoh's presence, they met Moses and Aaron as they were waiting for them. 21 They said to them, "May the LORD look upon you and judge you, for you have made us odious in Pharaoh's sight and in the sight of his servants, to put a sword in their hand to kill us."

No matter how you cut it, it appears to have looked to Moses like God failed. Either God didn't know what would happen, or God wasn't strong enough to win in the exchange.

Isn't that how we frame trouble a lot of the time? It didn't work out the way I thought it should. It doesn't seem like God's agenda got done. I did my part. It wasn't my fault. I parented properly. I stayed in the marriage. I worked hard at the job. Yet it failed. Where are you God? Why are you letting this happen? It never occurs to us that this may be what we need, even if it is not what we want!

A medical missionary to Africa told about how he forded many swift and bridgeless streams. The danger in crossing such streams lies in being swept off your feet and carried down-stream to greater depths and hurled to death on hidden rocks. He learned from the natives the best way to make such a hazardous crossing was to find a large stone (the heavier the better), lift it to your shoulder and carry it across the stream. The extra weight of the stone keeps your feet solid on the bed of the stream while crossing. While crossing the dangerous streams of life, we may need the ballast of burden bearing, a load of affliction, to keep us from being swept off our feet.

There are three responses that we should look at carefully, because they are highlighted in the verses.

First, consider the response of the Pharaoh: (5:6-9)

Increase the labor! One of the hardest results of any action you will ever take as a parent, a leader, or a boss is an action that causes pain and hardship on other people. As parents of older children, I find it increasingly harder to move from *protection* to *preparation,* yet that is exactly what we must do. God hadn't failed. His purposes were the same as before! Moses was not out of the will of God, and what appeared to be a failure was not at all!

God was at work on three levels here:

- Pharaoh and Egypt were being taught of the power and majesty of the God of Abraham. This would act in the generations to come as a deterrent to invasions.

- Moses was a leader still in the training stages. He was being shaped by God to do great things in the future by a patient God who needed to convince Moses to trust Him even when things didn't look hopeful!

- The children of Israel were also being trained to follow God. They needed to begin to recognize a life-long lesson that showed that God had a purpose in every trial.

Second, consider the response of the taskmasters: (5:10-19)

Only too happy to comply, these men were empowered to bring pain and hardship on others. It was easy for them to accuse the people of things that were not true. Note how they add to the statement of the laziness of the people in 5:17!

Someone has said, "Faith for my deliverance is not faith in God. Faith means, whether I am visibly delivered or not, I will stick to my belief that God is love. There are some things only learned in a fiery furnace." (*author unknown*)

As these new measures were levied on the people, I am sure that Moses was horrified to stand back and watch as the people's discouragement ensued. I'll bet even HE was discouraged. Yet, that was NOT the right response!

William Ward wrote: "Discouragement is dissatisfaction with the past, distaste for the present, and distrust of the future. It is ingratitude for the blessings of yesterday, indifference to the opportunities of today, and insecurity regarding strength for tomorrow. It is unawareness of the presence of beauty, unconcern for the needs of our fellowman, and unbelief in the promises of old. It is impatience with time, immaturity of thought, and impoliteness to God." (*Today in the Word*, April, 1989, p. 18)

Third and finally, consider the response of the foremen: (5:20-21).

As the people of God were brought low, they became embittered. They, too, were moving through the pain of disillusionment that Moses had failed. Unable to accept that it was God that failed, they simply turned all the pain to Moses and Aaron. Maybe they didn't really represent God as they said.

The surrender to failure can best be pictured by the foremen who would have accepted perpetual slavery over additional hardship for a season. They would have sunk back into their position of servitude rather than attain the calling of God for their people

What about us? Would we be willing to give up our comfort for God's purposes? Would we surrender things dear to us that God may use us and them more fully?

The Solution to Failure: (5:22-23)

Exodus 5:22 Then Moses returned to the LORD and said, "O Lord, why have You brought harm to this people? Why did You ever send me? 23 Ever since I came to Pharaoh to speak in Your name, he has done harm to this people, and You have not delivered Your people at all."

Moses asked the Lord two questions:

- Why did you bring harm to your people? The question behind the question is, "Are you a Good God?"

- Why did you send Me? Moses reacted to God's right to make him the instrument of this suffering! The real question is, "Do you have the right to do with me as You please?"

Moses concluded: You have failed to bring them out, so you have failed. It never occurred to him that God's purposes may not have been to do what Moses thought at this point in time! Pride lurks in our hearts on such a level that we truly believe we understand what we do not and cannot!

Success, for the believer, is doing what God tells you to do in His Word.

It is not measured by the response of anyone but God Himself. The only hands that we are called to desire a "clap" from are the nail scarred hands of our Savior. We cannot and dare not wait for everyone else to vote in favor of God's work before we commit ourselves. As new creatures in Christ, we are made to follow the voice of our Shepherd.

We must change the gauge of success from the outcome we want to the obedience God wants. The opportunity to obey is completely within our hands.

Walter B. Knight tells of an American tourist who had just seen the Passion Play. Approaching Mr. Lang who played the part of Christ, he asked, "May I be photographed with you while I lift your cross?" The tourist stooped to lift the cross but he couldn't. He exerted more energy, but still could not lift it. Looking at Mr. Lang, he said, "Your cross is certainly heavy!" Mr. Lang said, "Sir, I cannot represent Christ with a light cross!"

The University of Trouble?

Consider for a moment that God's Word also speaks about troubles for our learning:

1 Peter 5:10 After you have suffered for a little while, the God of all grace, who called you to His eternal glory in Christ, will Himself perfect, confirm, strengthen and establish you.

There are four things God wanted to do for them "after they had suffered a while."

- Perfect them: *kataridzo* is to fully **equip** and outfit one for life.
- Confirm them: *steridzo* is to **buttress** strength to withstand buffeting.
- Strengthen them: *stheno'-o* is to thicken girth to **fortify abilities**.
- Establish them: *themel-ee-o'-o* is to **lay** a deep and steady **foundation**.

Do you see it? God says we need suffering in our lives to be fully equipped, to find the outer supports and widening experiences that will make us strong. He says that the sufferings are the deep foundations of our lives that will bring us to the place where He can build much upon! We lie down and moan instead of seeing what God is really doing!

Someone once asked Paul Harvey, the journalist and radio commentator, to reveal the secret of his success. "I get up when I fall down," said Harvey.

As Abraham Lincoln prepared to sign the Emancipation Proclamation, he took his pen, moved it to the signature line, paused for a moment, and then dropped the pen. When asked why, the president replied, "If my name goes into history, it will be for this act, and if my hand trembles when I sign it, there will be some who will say, 'He hesitated.'" Lincoln then turned to the table, took up the pen, and boldly signed his name.

Are we ready to leave a trail of success? **To a believer, success is more about obedience than any external outcomes.**

Grasping God's Purpose: Lessons in Exodus

Lesson Seven: Exodus 6:1-13 "God of the Open Door"

When God directed Moses to Pharaoh and God also delivered trouble to Israel. The clear fact in the book of *Exodus* was that God both orchestrated the trouble and planned the result, a fact borne out by the statement in Exodus 3 that Pharaoh would not listen, but God would work. What does that mean? It means that God's intent was for Israel to go through trouble to teach them something they needed to know about Him and their walk with Him. There is nothing about this truth that is easy, but there is a comforting truth within this – that God had a plan through their suffering. When in the midst of the suffering, that is difficult to remember, but essential to rehearse.

Out of Exodus 5 the natural questions arise. The chapter ends with Moses asking two questions:

Exodus 5:22 Then Moses returned to the LORD and said, "O Lord, why have You brought harm to this people? Why did You ever send me? 23 Ever since I came to Pharaoh to speak in Your name, he has done harm to this people, and You have not delivered Your people at all."

What was he really asking God? The questions behind the questions are both profound and relevant to everyone who reads the ancient text today…

"Why did you bring harm to your people?" was actually the question: Are you really a good God**?**

If God is good, as the Scriptures claim: (Jesus said in *Luke 18:19 "No one is good except God alone*.") then why are the people you claim to care for (*Ex. 3:7: The Lord said, "I have surely seen the affliction of My people who are in Egypt, and have given heed to their cry because of their taskmasters, for I am aware of their sufferings."*) going through this suffering? Even though God thoroughly explained the purpose of the suffering in the same revelation that He offered the truth that he heard them –

followers of God only hear the part about the benefits and ignore or forget the troublesome part of the message.

Let me be clear: The issue of the Israelite suffering was no mystery. God promised them trouble and promised Moses rejection by Pharaoh in order to work the plan of creating fear in the heart of the Egyptians, and to fill the coffers of the Israelites on their way to the Promised Land. God has been no less clear that the path for a modern believer will run through pain to promise – but half the church denies it and many of the rest of us ignore it, acting like our time on Earth is supposed to be some precursor of the experiential blessings of Heaven.

God does bless us in this life, but His primary work is our transformation, not our comfort. These truths are about as welcome as making our brick quotas without precut straw to hold the mud together. Nevertheless, God tells the truth. God is good. God is working a plan, and God's people keep asking Him if He is truly good…

"Why did you send ME?" was actually the question: "Do you have the right to my life?"

The WHY question is linked with the rebellious root deep in our hearts. God allows us to question because He understands the fallen nature of man. Jesus knows what is in the hearts of His creation. The real issue of the WHY question is one of *rights of ownership*. Does God have the right to do as He pleases? If you want to make a group of American Christians really uncomfortable, read these words from God's Holy revelation:

Romans 9:14 What shall we say then? There is no injustice with God, is there? May it never be! 15 For He says to Moses, "I WILL HAVE MERCY ON WHOM I HAVE MERCY, AND I WILL HAVE COMPASSION ON WHOM I HAVE COMPASSION." 16 So then, it does not depend on the man who wills or the man who runs, but on God Who has mercy. 17 For the Scripture says to Pharaoh, "FOR THIS VERY PURPOSE I RAISED YOU UP, TO DEMONSTRATE MY POWER IN YOU, AND THAT MY NAME MIGHT BE PROCLAIMED THROUGHOUT THE WHOLE EARTH." 18 So then He has mercy on whom He desires, and He hardens whom He desires. 19 You will say to me then, "Why does He still find fault? For who resists His will?" 20 On the contrary, who are you, O man, who answers back to God? The thing molded will not say to the molder, "Why did you make me like this," will it? 21 Or does not the potter have a right over the clay, to make from the same lump one vessel for honorable use and another for common use? 22 What if God, although willing to demonstrate His wrath and to make His power known, endured with much patience vessels of wrath prepared for destruction? 23 And He did so to make known the riches of His glory upon vessels of mercy, which He prepared beforehand for glory, 24 even us, whom He also called, not from among Jews only, but also from among Gentiles.

Infantile Christianity desperately tries to construct a system of fairness and force God into that system - failing to understand four essential truths:

Biblically, God is good, but I am not.

Because of that I am not an effective arbiter of good and evil. My fallen nature is marred and self-serving to an extreme. God said:
Isaiah 55:9 For as the heavens are higher than the Earth, so are My ways higher than your ways and My thoughts than your thoughts.

Biblically, God is not arbitrary – but planned in His nature.

He doesn't just wind up the watch of history and let it go – He has a message to bring and a damsel to save. He is on a love quest. Within this quest, God's plan is deliberate:

Acts 2:23: ...this Man, delivered over by the predetermined plan and foreknowledge of God, you nailed to a cross by the hands of godless men and put Him to death.

Biblically, the path to blessing is through trouble.

That is the story of men like Abraham, Jacob, Joseph, Moses, Joshua, David, Hezekiah, Daniel and his friends, Jesus and His Disciples, Paul and virtually every prime mover of the literary story of the Bible.

Biblically, the measure of my life is in intimacy with Him.

Whether I pass through times of searing pain or sheer delight – the measure of my real success in life is about my intimate, yielded, unreserved love for Him – there is no other measure.
Follow the story of the questions for the next few verses and you will easily see the principle that oozes from the text like a salve on hurting hearts…

Key Principle: The depth of your relationship with God is directly connected to the depth of what doors in your heart you open to Him!

Why is this a salve? Because it places me back in the position of action amidst tough times, and strips away my victimization…Take a closer look:

Exodus 6:1 Then the LORD said to Moses, "Now you shall see what I will do to Pharaoh; for under compulsion he will let them go, and under compulsion he will drive them out of his land." 2 God spoke further to Moses and said to him, "I am the LORD; 3 and I appeared to Abraham, Isaac, and Jacob as God Almighty, but by My name, LORD, I did not make Myself known to them. 4 I also established My covenant with them, to give them the land of Canaan, the land in which they sojourned. 5 Furthermore, I have heard the groaning of the sons of Israel, because the Egyptians are holding them in bondage, and I have remembered My covenant. 6 Say, therefore, to the sons of Israel, 'I am the LORD, and I will bring you out from under the burdens of the Egyptians, and I will deliver you from their bondage. I will also redeem you with an outstretched arm and with great judgments. 7 Then I will take you for My people, and I will be your God; and you shall know that I am the LORD your God, Who brought you out from under the burdens of the Egyptians. 8 I will bring you to the land which I swore to give to Abraham, Isaac, and Jacob, and I will give it to you for a possession; I am the LORD.'" 9 So Moses spoke thus to the sons of Israel, but they did not listen to Moses on account of their despondency and cruel bondage. 10 Now the LORD spoke to Moses, saying, 11 "Go, tell Pharaoh king of Egypt to let the sons of Israel go out of his land." 12 But Moses spoke before the LORD, saying, "Behold, the sons of Israel have not listened to me; how then will Pharaoh listen to me, for I am unskilled in speech?" 13 Then the LORD spoke to Moses and to Aaron, and gave them a charge to the sons of Israel and to Pharaoh king of Egypt, to bring the sons of Israel out of the land of Egypt.

The text of Exodus 6 offers a rich and helpful backdrop to difficulty in our lives. If we look carefully, we will identify three principles of intimacy with God for our lives:

Principle 1: The NEED Principle:

The deeper your trouble – the more you will come to know the real ME as I truly am (says God – 6:1-6). The progression of these verse mirrors five basic objections that God overcame in Moses through the troubles:

Objection 1: I don't understand You, so this must not be Your will, and it isn't right for me (6:1).

Exodus 6:1 Then the LORD said to Moses, "Now you shall see what I will do to Pharaoh; for under compulsion he will let them go, and under compulsion he will drive them out of his land."

Three verbs tell the answer:

- (6:1a) Note: "You WILL learn My plan."
- (6:1b) Note: "Pharaoh WILL turn."
- (6:1b) Note: "Pharaoh will even WANT you to go in the end!"

There was a pastor, who after the usual Sunday evening hymns, stood up, walked over to the pulpit and, before he gave his sermon for the evening, briefly introduced a guest minister who was in the service that evening. In the introduction, the pastor told the congregation that the guest minister was one of his dearest childhood friends and that he wanted him to have a few moments to greet the church and share whatever he felt would be appropriate for the service. With that, an elderly man stepped up to the pulpit and began to speak. "A father, his son, and a friend of his were sailing off of the Pacific Coast," he began, "when a fast approaching storm blocked any attempt to get back to shore. The waves were so high, that even though the father was an experienced sailor, he could not keep the boat upright and the three were swept into the ocean as the boat capsized. The old man hesitated for a moment, making eye contact with two teenagers who were, for the first time since the service began, looking somewhat interested in his story. The aged minister continued with his story, "Grabbing a rescue line, the father had to make the most excruciating decision of his life: to which boy would he throw the other end of the lifeline. He only had seconds to make the decision. The father knew that his son was a Christian and he also knew that his son’s friend was not. The agony of his decision could not be matched by the torrent of waves. As the father yelled out, ‘I love you son!’ he threw out the lifeline to his son’s friend. By the time the father had pulled the friend back to the capsized boat, his son had disappeared beneath the raging swells into the black of the night. His body was never recovered."

By this time, the two teenagers were sitting up straight in the pew, anxiously waiting for the next words to come out of the old minister’s mouth. "The father," he continued, “knew his son would step into eternity with Jesus and could not bear the thought of his son’s friend stepping into eternity without Jesus. Therefore, he sacrificed his son to save his son’s friend…” With that the old man turned and sat back down in his chair as silence filled the room. The pastor again walked slowly to the pulpit and delivered a brief sermon…

Within minutes after the service ended, the two teenagers were at the old man’s side. "That was a nice story," politely stated the boys, "but I don’t think it was realistic for a father to give up his son’s life in hopes that the other boy would become a Christian." "Well, you’ve got a point there," the old man replied glancing down at the worn Bible. A big smile broadened his narrow face; he once again looked up at the boys and said, "It sure isn’t realistic, is it? But I’m standing today to tell you that the story gives me a glimpse of what it must have been like for God to give up His only son for me. You see… I was the father and your pastor was my son's friend."

How does verse one help us? It reminds us to look at the situation from the "after the fact" prospective. Was it better that God forced Israel into a hard situation? Yes, it was a process of bringing pain with purpose. God was opening Pharaoh's hands to offer them future blessing by initially closing them to temporary fists!

Objection 2: I don't control the process, so it is not good and not a blessing to me. (6:2). Note: "You will learn that I am Master."

Exodus 6:2 God spoke further to Moses and said to him, "I am the LORD…"

God was not the servant and Moses the Master – He is Lord and we are the servant. The prospect of someone ELSE being in charge is never easy – especially for someone who was raised with leadership potential as Moses was.

Objection 3: You ask a lot up front, and I struggle to trust you. (6:3-4).

We may not verbalize it, but many feel it:

Exodus 6:3 …and I appeared to Abraham, Isaac, and Jacob, as God Almighty, but by My name, LORD, I did not make Myself known to them. 4 I also established My covenant with them, to give them the land of Canaan, the land in which they sojourned.

- God replied: *I spoke to others, but you will know Me more intimately by My own Name!* (6:3). There was more of God to know that whole ears and unbroken hearts could not hear!

- What God had promised, He would not offer to those who did not trust Him through their pain (6:4)!

How deep a walk do you want? How much of the promise can you handle? "These are questions I can only show the answers to in your experience with Me," says God.

Objection 4: You don't respond WHEN I want, HOW I want. How can I truly trust You?

Exodus 6:5 Furthermore, I have heard the groaning of the sons of Israel, because the Egyptians are holding them in bondage, and I have remembered My covenant.

- *"You will see that I have heard you"* (6:5a).
- *"You will understand that I don't forget"* (6:5b).

At Ohio State University, Ravi Zaccharias did an open forum on a radio talk show. The host was an atheist. From the start, the callers were antagonistic. "I could feel the tension as soon as the lines lit up. One angry woman caller said, "All you people have is an agenda you're trying to promote." Referring to abortion, she said, "You want to take away our rights and invade our private lives." Abortion had not even been brought up. "Just a minute," I replied, "we didn't even raise the subject." "Ok," she said, "what is your position on abortion then?" I said, "Can I ask you a question? On every university campus I visit, somebody stands up and says that God is an evil God to allow all this evil into our world. This person typically says, 'A plane crashes: 30 people die, and 20 people live. What kind of God would arbitrarily choose some to live and some to die?'" I continued, "But when we play God and determine whether a child within a mother's womb should live, we argue for that as a moral right. So when human beings are given the privilege of playing God, it's called a moral right. When God plays God, we call it an immoral act. Can you justify this for me?" That was the end of the conversation.

Objection 5: I am afraid that I may be stuck out here alone!

Exodus 6:6 Say, therefore, to the sons of Israel, "I am the LORD, and I will bring you out from under the burdens of the Egyptians, and I will deliver you from their bondage. I will also redeem you with an outstretched arm and with great judgments."

- **Do what I say** before you receive what I promise (6:6a).
- Remember yourself, and remind others that **I have the right as your Master** (6:6b).
- **I will make measurable promises** that you will see progressively come to pass (6:6b).

One day Henry Ford was driving in the Michigan countryside when he came upon a man who's Model T had broken down. The guy was bent under the hood trying to figure what was wrong. Mr. Ford stopped and asked if he could take a look. In a few minutes, he had the car running. The grateful owner said, "I'm amazed at your ability; you fixed my car so easily." Ford replied, "I ought to be able to fix it, because I'm the one who designed it." The same is true with God—He designed us, and He can fix whatever's wrong with us.

The first principle was that of need – but it was followed by no less than five objections by Moses... Yet the text moves on. Note a second principle: what we can call "The Practice" Principle:

As you step out and obey, you begin to see God do what He has already promised He will do! (6:7-8).

Exodus 6:7 Then I will take you for My people, and I will be your God; and you shall know that I am the LORD your God, Who brought you out from under the burdens of the Egyptians. 8 I will bring you to the land which I swore to give to Abraham, Isaac, and Jacob, and I will give it to you for a possession; I am the LORD.

God offered Moses three things for the people:

- **Relationship**: I will take you for My people (7a);
- **Release**: I will deliver you! (6:6b);
- **Renewal**: I will give you back the things I had planned for you! (6:8).

Believers have these three things, but the world hasn't experienced them. We need to take God's love to them! It reminds me of the story:

One pastor wrote, "Esther, my wife, and I have a granddaughter named Zoe, the Greek word for life. She was born prematurely and weighed one pound, seven ounces, so small that my wedding ring could slide up her arm to her shoulder. The neonatologist who first examined her told us that she had a 5 to 10 percent chance of living three days. When Esther and I scrubbed up for our first visit and saw Zoe in her isolation chamber in the neonatal intensive care unit, she had two IVs in her navel, one in her foot, a monitor on each side of her chest, and a respirator tube and a feeding tube in her mouth. To complicate matters, Zoe's biological father had jumped ship the month before Zoe was born. Realizing this, a wise and caring nurse named Ruth gave me my instructions. 'For the next several months, at least, you're the surrogate father. I want you to come to the hospital every day to visit Zoe, and when you come, I want you to rub her body and her legs and arms with the tip of your finger. While you're caressing her, you should tell her over and over how much you love her, because she has to be able to connect your voice to your touch.' God knew that we also needed both His voice and His touch. So He gave us not only the Word but also His Son. And He gave us not only Jesus Christ but also His body, the Church. God's voice and touch say, 'I love you.'" (*sermon central illustrations*)

Principle 3: The Faith Principle:

You can't always see here and now what the plan is that God is working. Believe His promises and act according to His plans, and you will see more and more of His ways! Ex. 6:9-13.

Your first step may not be very strong, keep going!

Exodus 6:9 So Moses spoke thus to the sons of Israel, but they did not listen to Moses on account of their despondency and cruel bondage. 10 Now the LORD spoke to Moses, saying, 11 "Go, tell Pharaoh King of Egypt to let the sons of Israel go out of his land."

When I was a child, my minister father brought home a 12-year-old boy named Roger, whose parents had died from a drug overdose. There was no one to care for Roger, so my folks decided they'd just raise him as if he were one of their own sons. At first it was quite difficult for Roger to adjust to his new home—an environment free of heroin-addicted adults! Every day, several times a day, I heard my parents saying to Roger: "No, no. That's not how we behave in this family." "No, no. You don't have to scream or fight or hurt other people to get what you want." "No, no, Roger, we expect you to show respect in this family." And in time Roger began to change. Now, did Roger have to make all those changes in order to become a part of the family? No. He was made a part of the family simply by the grace of my father. But did he then have to do a lot of hard work because he was in the family? You bet he did. It was tough for him to change, and he had to work at it. But he was motivated by gratitude for the incredible love he had received. Do you have a lot of hard work to do now that the Spirit has adopted you into God's family? Certainly, but we do not work in order to become a son or a daughter of the heavenly Father. No, you make those changes because you are a son or daughter. And every time you start to revert back to the old addictions to sin, the Holy Spirit will say to you, "No, no. That's not how we act in this family."

Here is the point: Don't assume failure is measurable now! (6:12).

Exodus 6:12 But Moses spoke before the LORD, saying, "Behold, the sons of Israel have not listened to me; how then will Pharaoh listen to me, for I am unskilled in speech?" 13 Then the LORD spoke to Moses and to Aaron, and gave them a charge to the sons of Israel and to Pharaoh king of Egypt, to bring the sons of Israel out of the land of Egypt.

Failure is an opportunity for God to show us the net of Himself! A South-American preacher spoke of a conversation with a circus trapeze artist. The performer admitted the net underneath was there to keep them from breaking their necks, but added, "The net also keeps us from falling. Imagine there is no net. We would be so nervous that we would be more likely to miss and fall. If there wasn't a net, we would not dare to do some of the things we do. But because there's a net, we dare to make turns, and once I made three turns -- thanks to the net!"

Don't assume your victory is dependent on your ability (6:12)

What was God truly asking Moses to do? Was He asking him to convince Pharaoh? Was He calling Moses to release the people? No...

He was calling Moses to open his closed mind and heart and trust God. Why?

The depth of your relationship with God is directly connected to the depth of what doors in your heart you open to Him.

Grasping God's Purpose: Lessons in Exodus

Lesson Eight: Exodus 6:14-7:13 "The God that Will Be Known" (1)

People say that first impressions are really important.

Susan Boyle, age 47, took the stage at "Britain's Got Talent" (a television show) to sing "I Dreamed a Dream" from *Les Miserables*. Her first impression was stunningly mismatched to her ability. She looked somewhat unkept, dressed as one from a former time, and had the makeup sense of a woman stranded on a deserted island. She was stilted in movement, spoke in a halted fashion, and raised eyebrows of all of the judges before she performed – because of how poor the packaging appeared. In a few moments, the studio cued the music. What happened in the room was nothing short of a shocking transformation. Beauty poured from a disheveled vessel. Judges sat stunned. The crowd got the first wind of the woman's heavenly voice and was brought to their feet. Snickers were exchanged for clapping, and the judges were set back on their chairs utterly shocked at what they were hearing. Simon Cowell, Britain's favorite bad guy critic, could barely speak. The book was betrayed by the cover – but the book was too good to put down. Everyone in that room, on that particular day, was chastised without any word – for judging a book by its cover. Talent speaks louder than first impressions – but first impressions do count.

Without a doubt it is one of the truly epic scenes in the Bible. Moses and Aaron stand before Pharaoh's throne with all the trappings of Egyptian wealth and superiority around them. They brushed off desert dust, but on their best day they aren't that impressive. Between them they don't have a toothbrush, and considering the leeks and onions that were a part of the daily diet… that was surely a problem. What's more, they came bearing what I am sure seemed to them to be a "wonder stick" – a staff that could change form when God empowered it.

We don't need to guess at the Lord's purpose in the appearance of Moses and Aaron to Pharaoh – the text offers it clearly… in fact it keeps repeating it for the ensuing 10 plagues – God wanted to reveal Himself. The formula *"that you may know that I am the Lord"* or something similar to it appears eleven times (in Exodus 6:2, 6, 7, 8, 28; 7:5, 17; 8:10, 22; 9:14; and 10:2).

Key Principle: God wants people to know Him – and God wants His people to show Him who He is!

So what is the problem? We resist our mission. We fight God.
There are **six different ways we push aside His agenda**, and work against our own mission. We need to consider these six, as we reflect on whether we are allowing God to work through us. We choke off God's work when we don't examine and then yield in each area.

Resistance Point 1: Our Self Image

Exodus 6:14-22 sets up the characters for the stories that will follow in the desert. We unfolded the names of the grandsons of Jacob through three of his sons – Reuben, Simeon and Levi. We "zero in" on Amram and his sons - Moses and Aaron. The whole list of thirty-five names boiled down to this:

God doesn't choose celebrities – He chooses **ordinary sinful and weak** men and women to do His bidding. These men and the families they bore were not super spiritual. Quite the contrary – they were often a mess. God doesn't choose people because they are "better specimens of obedience" – but because He desired to do so. He is working a plan…

And He can use you! I don't need to hear about your past, or your "special needs." If you are, open, God is open for Heaven's business through your life. We cannot put it off – the challenge for our openness is absolute.

God uses the man or woman who sees past themselves and trusts that God is able to do exceedingly abundantly above what they think or can verbalize.

Resistance Point 2: Our Availability

Hand in hand with the point of self-image is a second truth - God shows His power most powerfully to those who let Him. God isn't pushy. We can resist God's desire to use us. We can kick against Him when He wants to do something powerful in and through us

.

When Moses and Aaron made themselves available, God spoke through them powerfully. God promised:

Exodus 7:1 Then the LORD said to Moses, "See, I make you as God to Pharaoh, and your brother Aaron shall be your prophet."

We don't have to follow God – even as believers. Yet, when we don't, we choke off our own blessing. We throttle down our own effectiveness. What do you want to be able to say you were to the people in your life – one that drew others to God or one who apologized for your beliefs?

I read this a few days ago from the *Associates for Biblical Research Blog* and it reminded me of what we are facing across the nation as we move from a biblical world view to a man- made explanation of things:

As soon as I saw his reaction, I knew what had happened to him! He was concerned about associating with a ministry that fully believes in the inerrancy of the Bible, and promotes its reliability and authority from the first verse of Genesis to the last verse of Revelation. But I was concerned that his current associations with compromised Christian academics were poisoning his pure devotion to Jesus Christ and to the Word of God. You see, at his "Christian" college the professors taught him … the Flood was not universal but local; Adam and Eve were not the first humans on Earth; and much of the history of Israel is not historical and cannot be accepted as true. But of course, he believed in Jesus and even in the Resurrection—but for the life of me I don't know why! He had already accepted the egregious compromises of secularized "Christian" academics for most of biblical history, so I wondered if by hanging on to Jesus it was just a fire insurance policy for his soul! The conversation was a tragedy. This young man's mind and his direction in life were ruined not by secularists and atheists, but by professing Christians. Why should we be surprised? Isn't that the same spiritual disease that was spread to him from his professors?

They had compromised years before by rejecting the plain teaching of Scripture, exchanging for it the philosophies of men. Professors had replaced Revelation with human Reason and declared that they knew better than God how the Earth was formed, how life began, and how man was to live on the Earth, and who redefined in modern terms what must have happened in the past... .The Church and its educational "system" have all too often turned men and women against the Bible. The Church has taught them to be embarrassed by what the Bible plainly says. ... Instead of worrying about what colleagues will think or about one's academic acceptability before peers, we should be far more concerned about what God thinks of us! Jesus knew that people could pretend to follow Him, but the proof of their discipleship would be shown by how they responded to His teaching—His words—and to all of the words of Scripture. To be ashamed of His words is to be ashamed of Him. Tragically, that is where many professing Christians are today..."

When God promised to make Moses as God to Pharaoh, He wasn't making a small and private bargain. We can have a huge effect on the people of our lives if we will stand for His truth in our hearts, with our minds, and in our actions.

God uses the available person, not the "special" person. God uses the one that really believes what God says.

Resistance Point 3: Our Focus

When Moses and Aaron limited their message to what God told them to speak, they kept the message clear and strong.
Exodus 7:2 You shall speak all that I command you, and your brother Aaron shall speak to Pharaoh that he let the sons of Israel go out of his land. 3 But I will harden Pharaoh's heart that I may multiply My signs and My wonders in the land of Egypt.

Look again at 7:2-3. Moses was commanded to stay focused on the message God gave. He wasn't to get too far ahead. God would supply when the time came to grow, expand and move out. For the moment, he was to speak only the message God told him to – and wait for God to move mountains.

I was reading just this week about the director of the George Muller Foundation who told of God's perfect timing in the provision of guidance and resources.

The Foundation had been requested to commence a new child-care project which would require a great commitment in time and resources. The trustees decided that they couldn't go ahead unless they received clear direction from the Lord, and so they committed the need to God in prayer. The day came for a decision to be made, but no definite leading had been received. Then on the day of their meeting a substantial sum was received from a donor earmarked for such a project - and what was more remarkable was that the gift had been designated over 20 years before but because of legal problems over the estate it had just become available.

God uses people who keep their focus on what He declares, and vibrantly offers water from the well provided by God alone. He knows the real needs, and He asks us to stay on message.

Resistance Point 4: Out Foundation

Discouragement can wipe out the ranks faster than a bad flu. Discouragement sets in when the gap between our expectations and reality becomes our focal point. How do we keep from being overwhelmed with discouragement?

When Moses and Aaron believed God's prophetic truth, they were able to continue in the face of apparent failure.

Exodus 7: 4 When Pharaoh does not listen to you, then I will lay My hand on Egypt and bring out My hosts, My people the sons of Israel, from the land of Egypt by great judgments.

Newscaster Paul Harvey told a remarkable story of God's providential care over thousands of allied prisoners during World War II, many of whom were Christians. One of America's mighty bombers took off from the island of Guam headed for Kokura, Japan, with a deadly cargo. Because clouds covered the target area, the sleek B-29 circled for nearly an hour until its fuel supply reached the danger point. The captain and his crew, frustrated because they were right over the primary target yet not able to fulfill their mission, finally decided they had better go for the secondary target. Changing course, they found that the sky was clear. The command was given, "Bombs away!" and the B-29 headed for its home base. Sometime later an officer received some startling information from military intelligence. Just one week before that bombing mission, the Japanese had transferred one of their largest concentrations of captured Americans to the city of Kokura. Upon reading this, the officer exclaimed, "Thank God for that protecting cloud! If the city hadn't been hidden from the bomber, it would have been destroyed and thousands of American boys would have died." God's ways are behind the scenes; but He moves all the scenes which He is behind. We have to learn this, and let Him work!

I love that story because it reminds me that God has a reason for delays, changes, and moves from above the board. I can't see the play. I only see part of the board. God sees it all! When Moses rested on God's promises, he relaxed about the bends in the road.

Discouragement became a secondary concern, because following God was the primary one. We fall to discouragement when we take on our shoulders the success of God's plan – that is not our call.

We serve at the pleasure of our King – and success is His problem… Obedience is ours.

Resistance Point 5: Our Vision

When Moses and Aaron saw the vision of God's long-term plan, they could take courage and know that what they were doing was a high calling – making known their Master.

Exodus 7:5 "The Egyptians shall know that I am the LORD when I stretch out My hand on Egypt and bring out the sons of Israel from their midst." 6 So Moses and Aaron did it; as the LORD commanded them, thus they did. 7 Moses was eighty years old and Aaron eighty-three, when they spoke to Pharaoh.

Let me ask you: "Who are people seeing when they look at your life? Are they viewing a life in transformation or a mess with excuses? Can they see in your actions a distinct form of Jesus Christ.? Do your values reflect Jesus' values? Do you look and act like a Christian on Tuesday afternoon at a business meeting, or Thursday morning at the gym?"

Moses was not responsible for Pharaoh's change of heart or repentance. Moses was responsible for exactly what all of us are responsible for – yielded obedience in the work of reflecting God to a lost world.

Natural man cannot understand the thrill of sharing the truth about Who God is! They don't get it, and it isn't their fault.

"Every animal on Earth has a set of senses that corresponds with the environment around it, and some of those senses far exceed ours. Humans can perceive only thirty percent of the range of the sun's light and 1/70th of the spectrum of electromagnetic energy. Many animals exceed our abilities. Bats detect insects by sonar; pigeons navigate by magnetic fields; bloodhounds perceive a world of smell unavailable to us. Perhaps the spiritual or "unseen" world requires an inbuilt set of senses activated only through some sort of spiritual quickening. 'No one can see the kingdom of God without being born from above,' said Jesus. 'The man without the Spirit does not accept the things that come from the Spirit of God, for they are foolishness to him, and he cannot understand them, because they are spiritually discerned,' said Paul. Both expressions point to a different level of correspondence available only to a person spiritually alive." (Citation: Philip Yancey, *Seeing the Invisible God: Books and Culture*, May/June 2000, p.8)

If we truly believe what God has said about our mission, we will be ready to sacrifice to make it happen. **We stand at the edge of eternal life or death with a message that can change anyone who will open their heart**. God has promised some are going to open. We must keep our eye on His mission – that is the vision we must have. **Distraction of other visions blurs what God called us to be and do**.

Don't forget, it isn't just about what we do, it is about our dependence on God to do what we cannot. If we truly believe we serve the God of the Universe and nothing is too difficult for Him – then our prayers should be reflecting this.

I love this true story: A woman came to a missionary at Bengalore, India, asking him to interfere and prevent a certain native Christian from praying for her any more. When asked how she knew that the Christian was praying for her, she replied, "I used to perform my worship to the idols quite comfortably, but for some time past I have not been able to do so. Besides, he told me at the time that he was praying for my family, and now my son and two daughters have become Christians. If he goes on praying, he may make me, too, become a Christian. He is always bringing things to pass with his prayers. Somebody must make him stop.

Read verse five one more time: *"The Egyptians SHALL KNOW THAT I AM THE LORD."* God was not asking anything, He was stating the future. It is a secure future when God declares it to be such.

Philippians 2:8b He humbled Himself by becoming obedient to the point of death, even death on a cross. 9 For this reason also, God highly exalted Him, and bestowed on Him the name which is above every name, 10 so that at the name of Jesus EVERY KNEE WILL BOW, of those who are in Heaven and on Earth and under the Earth, 11 and that every tongue will confess that Jesus Christ is Lord, to the glory of God the Father.

We must understand that our call to show men and women the passage from death to life is an exciting and powerful call in the hands of the obedient.

It is what brings the weight of the attack of the enemy upon us. He has everything to fear if we faithfully follow – and that truth is one that must be kept in our eyes – the vision of a high calling of priesthood to a lost world.

Resistance Point 6: Our Persistence

The last point that can choke off the flow of God's work through us is simple discouragement. We can become despondent. How does it happen? Sometimes it occurs because we were insufficiently trained in the Word to really handle the struggles of walking with God in a lost world. Once it got hard, we found ourselves floundering for answers.

Beat down, we just grind to a halt. Look at the persistence of two men standing in Pharaoh's court:

Exodus 7:8 Now the LORD spoke to Moses and Aaron, saying, 9 "When Pharaoh speaks to you, saying, 'Work a miracle,' then you shall say to Aaron, 'Take your staff and throw it down before Pharaoh, that it may become a serpent.'" 10 So Moses and Aaron came to Pharaoh, and thus they did just as the LORD had commanded; and Aaron threw his staff down before Pharaoh and his servants, and it became a serpent. 11 Then Pharaoh also called for the wise men and the sorcerers, and they also, the magicians of Egypt, did the same with their secret arts. 12 For each one threw down his staff and they turned into serpents. But Aaron's staff swallowed up their staffs. 13 Yet Pharaoh's heart was hardened, and he did not listen to them, as the LORD had said.

It was a cool moment when the staff of Moses was tossed on the floor and became a snake. The audience gasped in amazement. For a second, a quick smirk formed on Moses' face. Pharaoh's eyes got big. The problem was that Pharaoh was a well-educated politician. He wasn't going to let them see him sweat. He lifted his hand to his face and whispered to an aide. Out the servant went. In came the magicians and sorcerers. Now the whole floor was full of snakes! Moses quit smirking…. Then God made a move. His snake gobbled up one after another of the competitor's snakes. God doesn't get upstaged when He is making a point!

Bill Hybels tells about an interesting experience after a baptism service in their church. He writes: "I bumped into a woman in the stairwell who was crying. I thought this was a little odd, since the service was so joyful. I asked her if she was all right. She said, 'No, I'm struggling.' She said, 'My mom was baptized today. I prayed for her every day for almost 20 years. The reason I'm crying is because I came this close to giving up on her. At the 5-year mark I said, "Who needs this? God isn't listening." At the 10-year mark I said, "Why am I wasting my breath?" At the 15-year mark I said, "This is absurd." At the 19-year mark I said, "I'm just a fool." But I just kept trying, kept praying. Even with weak faith I kept praying. Then she gave her life to Christ, and she was baptized today.'"

If you don't have a strong persistence, your power will falter when challenged.

"We've all heard about Thomas Edison who performed 10,000 experiments before he perfected the incandescent light. He believed, and he persisted despite 9,999 failed attempts. You may know of Paul Ehrlich, who tried 605 possible remedies for syphilis. He received the Nobel Prize for his success on attempt number 606. He believed in a remedy for syphilis." (*sermon central*)

We must remember that although a great many fakes and forgeries exist, there is still but one true message of salvation – and it is found in the blood of Jesus. That idea has been waning in the voice of the modern church… but one writer reminds us that it cannot and must not. We must be true and persistent to the message God has called us to.

E.B. White's comment: "People have re-cut their clothes to follow the fashion. People have remodeled their ideas, too. They have taken in their convictions a little at the waist, shortened the sleeves of their resolve, and fitted themselves out in a new intellectual ensemble copied from a smart design out of the very latest page of history."

Jesus reminds us to be faithful in speaking the truth concerning Him!

Matthew 10:32: Therefore, everyone who confesses Me before men, I will also confess him before My Father Who is in Heaven. 33 But whoever denies Me before men, I will also deny him before My Father Who is in Heaven

We need to recognize that some of us will stand accused of blinding men's eyes by marring the view they have of God if we don't get serious. We don't walk in guilt, but we DO need to seriously examine our testimony today.

Remember, **only when we reflect God as He truly is, will people be able to respond to Him as they should! The catch? He has chosen to be seen, primarily, through our lives!**

Grasping God's Purpose: Lessons in Exodus

Lesson Nine: Exodus 7:14-11:10 "The God that Will Be Known" (2)

In the ancient world, the way to spell "power" was "PHARAOH." His throne personified the ability to erect great monuments, amass vast armies, organize elaborate rituals, or spin colorful tales in writing on the huge walls of ancient temples and tombs. How shocking that an elderly shepherd and his brother could change all that, because they brought the truth about the Creator of all things.

Key Principle: God wants people to know Him – and God wants His people to show Him who He is! When God is truly seen, men know the truth – they cannot trust any other beside Him.

Years ago Warren Wiersbe reminded us that God has been masked by the enemy of our souls, and only when He is unmasked and seen as He truly is, will we understand how to respond! We have seen in the past that when the enemy was at work, it was always to move men from seeing God as He is, to seeing something other than Him:

Eve: Satan entered the Garden of Eden to make her **ignorant** of God's will in her life. "Has God really said?" was the pitch he made… questioning God's veracity in His Word to move her to disobedience. If he could get Eve to believe God was holding back on her the best things, he could entice her to mutiny. **Satan wants us to think that God is holding us from having real fun and real joy.**

Job: Satan entered the throne room of Heaven and sought permission to challenge Job's health and strength so that he would make Job **impatient** with God's will – through the harassment of suffering and pain of loss. If he could get Job to believe that God was not good, Job would mutiny.

Satan wants us to believe that God isn't really good.

David: In the Chronicles we read of Satan coming to King David and stirring him up to believe that his position was being held by his own means. He was enticed to count the people in a census. Joab warned him to abandon the count and remember that God was the One that held David's throne in his hands. The enemy attempted to get David to walk **independent** of God's will, thereby creating yet another mutiny.

Satan wants us to believe we don't really need God's direction to be successful.

Zechariah: In the third chapter of his prophecy we read a time when the enemy showed Zechariah an apparition of Joshua the High Priest all soiled and dirty. His attempt was to undermine the work of God and lay an **indictment** against God's appointed leader. If he could get the people to see that the men they were called to follow had flaws, he could get them to cease listening to God's instruction and create a mutiny.

Satan wants us to see everything that is wrong with the messenger, so we reject the message God is speaking.

I repeat this lesson because as we face openly the account of Moses before Pharaoh, we must understand this was not a flesh and blood contest. Heaven and Hell were struggling against one another in a profound way – just as is happening in your life. You may not see it, but your problems are not as simple as they may appear

You are not simply wrestling against memories of your past – but against an enemy that only wants to recall the memories that will help you rebel or feel abused and abandoned. You are being enticed to mutiny your God and your faith by feeling bad about your past.

You are not simply wrestling against a set of circumstances that seems to work against you – a car that keeps breaking down when you cannot afford it to, an hourly cut back when you are on the brink of financial disaster, an illness that makes work twice as hard. You are being beckoned to mutiny because of the problems of your present.

You are not simply caught in a relationship with a vindictive boss with his or her issues, or a landlord that is stirred up in his life and cannot seem to keep his problems off your front step – though you pay on time and keep the property in good shape. You are being drawn away from your walk with God because of the problems with people.

You are not simply struggling to move forward in spite of tendencies to get sidetracked and distracted, you are wrestling against forces that play on your personality traits to keep you from following the Master that bought you!

You are in a spiritual war that is being played out on the chessboard of your physical life. It is painful, challenging and powerfully disguised… but the Word of God is clear

Ephesians 6:10 says: Finally, be strong in the Lord and in the strength of His might. 11 Put on the full armor of God, so that you will be able to stand firm against the schemes of the devil. 12 For our struggle is not against flesh and blood, but against the rulers, against the powers, against the world forces of this darkness, against the spiritual forces of wickedness in the heavenly places.

Stop now and count the enemies Paul exposed to the Ephesians:

- **Schemes** of the wicked one. The enemy is plotting to bring you down.
- **Spiritual rulers**. There are voices beckoning to rule people in our world.
- **Powers**. There are those who were granted greater authority that are wicked at heart.
- **World forces of darkness**. There are those who are pushing to tear down the good.
- **Spiritual forces of wickedness**. There are powerful spiritual dark forces behind the scenes.

Believers who ignore these truths, or forget them are already part way into the ensnaring of the enemy. Paul revealed to the Ephesians something that is easy for every believer to forget – this battle is against spiritual forces. Let me invoke you to peer back into the past and see how this battle played out for one of our flawed but favored spiritual fathers of the past – Moses

.

As we watch the story, look at three areas:

First, keep your eyes on **how God worked in three different people**, because they are examples of people you know…

There are three players: people or groups of people that have the opportunity to know the Lord in the drama of the plagues:

- Moses (representing the **strong believer**)
- The Israelites (representing the **weak but growing believers**)
- Egyptians and Pharaoh (representing the **unbeliever**)

Second, note that the **story offers internally one purpose:** The Lord's purpose in the 10 plagues is **to reveal Himself.** The formula " . *that you may know that I am the Lord.,"* or something similar to it appears eleven times (in Exodus 6:2, 6, 7, 8, 28; 7:5, 17; 8:10, 22; 9:14; and 10:2).

Third, recognize three patterns: The story offers a way for God to show some important **distinctions** God makes with people. Doesn't God see all people the same? NO! God distinguishes.

Now, let's take a close look at the story and see what God says He is trying to do and how He teaches about Himself:

1st Plague: Water to Blood (Exodus 7:14-19).

Both the Nile and stored water was affected

Exodus 7:14 Then the LORD said to Moses, "Pharaoh's heart is stubborn; he refuses to let the people go. 15 Go to Pharaoh in the morning as he is going out to the water, and station yourself to meet him on the bank of the Nile; and you shall take in your hand the staff that was turned into a serpent. 16 You shall say to him, 'The LORD, the God of the Hebrews, sent me to you, saying, "Let My people go, that they may serve Me in the wilderness. But behold, you have not listened until now.' 17 Thus says the LORD, 'By this you shall know that I am the LORD: behold, I will strike the water that is in the Nile with the staff that is in my hand, and it will be turned to blood. 18 The fish that are in the Nile will die, and the Nile will become foul, and the Egyptians will find difficulty in drinking water from the Nile.'" 19 Then the LORD said to Moses, "Say to Aaron, 'Take your staff and stretch out your hand over the waters of Egypt, over their rivers, over their streams, and over their pools, and over all their reservoirs of water, that they may become blood; and there will be blood throughout all the land of Egypt, both in vessels of wood and in vessels of stone.'"

God's judgment was upon at least three different gods and their respective followers:

Hapi – the god of the Nile
Anqet -- the goddess who was a water goddess
Khnemu -- the god who was an ancient water god and one of Egypt's oldest known gods

Egypt worshipped the Nile god as their daily source of life and sustenance since it was the waters of the Nile that watered their crops and gave them water that was necessary for drinking, cleaning, and bathing. Now that life-giving water carried nothing but death. Today, God would stretch the hand of Moses against the dollar that we worship to provide us with all the needs of life. Their Nile is our Wall Street, our Consumer Price Index, our source of daily need meeting…the dollar has become a source of worship for many in our land. **Know this: It cannot be trusted!**

2nd Plague: Frogs Everywhere! (Exodus 8:1-15)

Exodus 8:1 Then the LORD said to Moses, "Go to Pharaoh and say to him, 'Thus says the LORD, "Let My people go, that they may serve Me. 2 But if you refuse to let them go, behold, I will smite your whole territory with frogs. 3 The Nile will swarm with frogs, which will come up and go into your house and into your bedroom and on your bed, and into the houses of your servants and on your people, and into your ovens and into your kneading bowls. 4 So the frogs will come up on you and your people and all your servants."'" 5 Then the LORD said to Moses, "Say to Aaron, 'Stretch out your hand with your staff over the rivers, over the streams and over the pools, and make frogs come up on the land of Egypt.'" 6 So Aaron stretched out his hand over the waters of Egypt, and the frogs came up and covered the land of Egypt. 7 The magicians did the same with their secret arts, making frogs come up on the land of Egypt. 8 Then Pharaoh called for Moses and Aaron and said, "Entreat the LORD that He remove the frogs from me and from my people; and I will let the people go, that they may sacrifice to the LORD." ...13 The LORD did according to the word of Moses, and the frogs died out of the houses, the courts, and the fields. 14 So they piled them in heaps, and the land became foul. 15 But when Pharaoh saw that there was relief, he hardened his heart and did not listen to them, as the LORD had said.

The frogs were a judgment against "Heqt" – a frog headed goddess that represented the resurrection of the dead of Egypt. Frogs were considered a daily source of general comfort to the Egyptians because the frogs would not only carry a symbolism of life after death but the frogs would eat the flies that often troubled the land, but God turned that "blessing" into a curse. Frogs were a source of comfort for the people – a way of keeping the flies at bay and offering them the quiet hope of an afterlife. They were a symbol of religious life in the time that helped people cope and hope. They were like the smooth tongues of preachers of the "feel good church" that has covered our airwaves. Picture your favorite frog...they are riding in beautiful automobiles and offering hope and a "no cost" relationship with God. **Know this: They cannot be trusted!**

3rd Plague: Lice, Sand Flea or Chigger Infestation (Exodus 8:16-19)

Exodus 8:16 Then the LORD said to Moses, "Say to Aaron, 'Stretch out your staff and strike the dust of the Earth, that it may become gnats through all the land of Egypt.'" 17 They did so; and Aaron stretched out his hand with his staff, and struck the dust of the Earth, and there were gnats on man and beast. All the dust of the Earth became gnats through all the land of Egypt. 18 The magicians tried with their secret arts to bring forth gnats, but they could not; so there were gnats on man and beast. 19 Then the magicians said to Pharaoh, "This is the finger of God." But Pharaoh's heart was hardened, and he did not listen to them, as the LORD had said.

The infestation was a judgment against "Kheper" – the god of insects.

Again, the God of Abraham stepped up further his attack on a daily source of comfort – but this time it became much more personal in the discomfort. It is like our air-conditioning or a calamine lotion when you itch. **Know this: Your personal comforts cannot be trusted to keep you well. Sickness will come. Your body will age. Those who don't know it will find it out.**

4th Plague: Flies Everywhere! (Exodus 8:20-32)

Exodus 8:20 Now the LORD said to Moses, "Rise early in the morning and present yourself before Pharaoh, as he comes out to the water, and say to him, 'Thus says the LORD, "Let My people go, that they may serve Me. 21 For if you do not let My people go, behold, I will send swarms of flies on you and on your servants and on your people and into your houses; and the houses of the Egyptians will be full of swarms of flies, and also the ground on which they dwell. 22 But on that day I will set apart the land of Goshen, where My people are living, so that no swarms of flies will be there, in order that you may know that I, the LORD, am in the midst of the land. 23 I will put a division between My people and your people. Tomorrow this sign will occur."'"

This may well have attacked a superstition of the scarab gods and amulets that were abundant in the day. This appears to be a warning that the superstitions of the people were being cast aside! The scarab offered good luck. It was similar to the way people view their horoscope, a fortune cookie, or a broken mirror. It is the peering of a superstition of the past into their lives. They "knock on wood" or refuse to pass below a ladder. **Know this: Your superstitions don't change spiritual realities. You cannot trust the stars or some inner voice – God has a Word and it is not found there.**

5th Plague: Death of the Livestock (Exodus 9:1-7)

Exodus 9:3 "...behold, the hand of the LORD will come with a very severe pestilence on your livestock which are in the field, on the horses, on the donkeys, on the camels, on the herds, and on the flocks. 4 But the LORD will make a distinction between the livestock of Israel and the livestock of Egypt, so that nothing will die of all that belongs to the sons of Israel." 5 The LORD set a definite time, saying, "Tomorrow the LORD will do this thing in the land."

This targeted the god Hap, also known by his Greek designation "Apis." Symbolized by a sacred bull, this may be a take-off from the Minoan civilization of ancient Crete.

The plague eroded the long term stability of the economy of Egypt. Cattle especially were seen as a symbol of wealth. For us today, it would probably be best equivalent to our housing market, where most Americans have the majority of their wealth on the balance sheet. **Know this: Your market value CANNOT be the source of your trust - I don't have to convince you how quickly the value unravels in the face of adversity.**

6th Plague: Boils on the Egyptian People and Animals not killed with the livestock. (Exodus 9:8-12)

Exodus 9:8 Then the LORD said to Moses and Aaron, "Take for yourselves handfuls of soot from a kiln, and let Moses throw it toward the sky in the sight of Pharaoh. 9 It will become fine dust over all the land of Egypt, and will become boils breaking out with sores on man and beast through all the land of Egypt."

God's judgment of what was likely "skin anthrax" targeted their belief in "Imhotep" the physician god, and "Thoth" (the god of magic and healing).

Known medicines could relieve the pain and suffering. The God of Abraham stood above the education and technology of Egypt to solve their problems.

Know this: We cannot educate America out of its troubles. Educated pagans will create yet more oppression and trouble.

7th plague: Hail (Exodus 9:13-35)

Exodus 918 "Behold, about this time tomorrow, I will send a very heavy hail, such as has not been seen in Egypt from the day it was founded until now. 19 Now therefore send, bring your livestock and whatever you have in the field to safety. Every man and beast that is found in the field and is not brought home, when the hail comes down on them, will die." 20 The one among the servants of Pharaoh who feared the word of the LORD made his servants and his livestock flee into the houses; 21 but he who paid no regard to the word of the LORD left his servants and his livestock in the field...

This targeted the confidence in the goddess Nut the goddess of the sky.

The hail affected every plant, tree, and living thing in Egypt that was covered or protected. The short-term economy or "daily market" economy was trampled, while God did not destroy the whole of the food supply chain. In the short run, there would be hunger, but it would not destroy Egypt's ability to rebound.

Know this: Your job is not the solution to your troubles. It cannot produce all you need. It will not last.

8th Plague: The Locusts (Exodus 10:1-20)

Exodus 10: 4 "For if you refuse to let My people go, behold, tomorrow I will bring locusts into your territory. 5 They shall cover the surface of the land, so that no one will be able to see the land. They will also eat the rest of what has escaped—what is left to you from the hail—and they will eat every tree which sprouts for you out of the field. 6 Then your houses shall be filled and the houses of all your servants and the houses of all the Egyptians, something which neither your fathers nor your grandfathers have seen, from the day that they came upon the Earth until this day." And he turned and went out from Pharaoh. 7 Pharaoh's servants said to him, "How long will this man be a snare to us? Let the men go, that they may serve the LORD their God. Do you not realize that Egypt is destroyed?" ...12 Then the LORD said to Moses, "Stretch out your hand over the land of Egypt for the locusts that they may come up on the land of Egypt and eat every plant of the land, even all that the hail has left." ... 15 For they covered the surface of the whole land, so that the land was darkened; and they ate every plant of the land and all the fruit of the trees that the hail had left. Thus nothing green was left on tree or plant of the field through all the land of Egypt."

This targeted belief in the god Seth, the protector of crops.

The locusts must have eaten whatever crops or vegetation was covered from the hail. Whatever security the Egyptians felt from the ability to protect cucumbers, leeks and the like from the hail was stripped from them as the God of Abraham crushed the remaining daily market items. This plague seems to have targeted the HOPE of the Egyptian people, as God stuck deeper and deeper.

Know this: No political leader can offer real hope. The machine is too big, and the disappointment follows the failed expectations.

9th Plague: Plague of Darkness (Exodus 10:21-29)

Exodus 10:21 Then the LORD said to Moses, "Stretch out your hand toward the sky, that there may be darkness over the land of Egypt, even a darkness which may be felt." 22 So Moses stretched out his hand toward the sky, and there was thick darkness in all the land of Egypt for three days. 23 They did not see one another, nor did anyone rise from his place for three days, but all the sons of Israel had light in their dwellings…

This appears to have been a high altitude dust covering of "loess soil" (see Ex. 10:21 "felt") that tore away confidence in the powerful "Ra", one thought to have been the most powerful of the gods – the sun god. Special cultic ceremonies also existed for Khepera, the god of the rising sun (lit. "comes into being"), and Atum, the god of the setting sun (lit. "complete one"). They had dust storms before and since, but not stationary ones that affected only one part of the land for three days! This plague DEMORALIZED the people and left them feeling powerless! **Know this: No matter how powerful and ingenious men are, their lives are dependent on things they do not control.**

10th Plague: Death of the Firstborn Children and protected cattle (Exodus 11:1-10)

Exodus 11:1 Now the LORD said to Moses, "One more plague I will bring on Pharaoh and on Egypt; after that he will let you go from here. When he lets you go, he will surely drive you out from here completely. …" 4 Moses said, "Thus says the LORD, 'About midnight I am going out into the midst of Egypt, 5 and all the firstborn in the land of Egypt shall die, from the firstborn of the Pharaoh who sits on his throne, even to the firstborn of the slave girl who is behind the millstones; all the firstborn of the cattle as well. 6 Moreover, there shall be a great cry in all the land of Egypt, such as there has not been before and such as shall never be again. 7 But against any of the sons of Israel a dog will not even bark, whether against man or beast that you may understand how the LORD makes a distinction between Egypt and Israel."

This terrible plague destroyed the confidence of the people in the god Bes the "Protector of Children" or "Protector of The Family."

It further eroded confidence in the "Ka" or "life force" of the Egyptians. **Know this: Your family is vulnerable to forces beyond your control. If you place your confidence in your children, you will face deep disappointment.**

So what have we learned that God showed the people in our story?

You can't trust the daily source of your sustenance of the past; or the source of your comfort and personal relief. Your superstitions are worthless and your economy a house of cards. Your education, health care and technology can't save you from God's power, nor can you have confidence that your leaders will be able to remain strong in the face of the troubles. Your family is vulnerable.

What can I trust? Where can I find hope ? Other gods are merely the creations of human imagining. As much as people may try to think of ways of expressing their ideas of God, there is no substitute for the real thing. There's no substitute for the revelation of God that He has given us in His Word and now in the person of his Son, Jesus.

Long ago He spoke a word through the prophet Amos in 5:3-6 3 For thus says the Lord GOD, "The city which goes forth a thousand strong will have a hundred left, and the one which goes forth a hundred strong will have ten left to the house of Israel." 4 For thus says the LORD to the house of Israel, "Seek Me that you may live. 5 But do not resort to Bethel, and do not come to Gilgal, nor cross over to Beersheba; for Gilgal will certainly go into captivity and Bethel will come to trouble. 6 Seek the LORD that you may live, or He will break forth like a fire, O house of Joseph, and it will consume with none to quench it for Bethel..."

When God is truly seen, men know the truth – they cannot trust any other beside Him.

Grasping God's Purpose: Lessons in Exodus

Lesson Ten: Exodus 7-12
"The God that Will Be Known" (3)

When we left off in our story in the biblical account of the Exodus, we were standing on a hill overlooking the ancient cities of *Pithom* and *Ramses* in Egypt. We were watching a drama play out between three men. First in our scene was the mighty ruler of Egypt, the Pharaoh of the most powerful nation of his day. He was a world leader with unparalleled strength on his continent -- a man groomed for destiny. Standing before him, day after day, were two old men, neither powerfully dressed nor imposing in their appearance. One was dressed, in fact, in the garb of a Midianite shepherd. The other stood before Pharaoh with the meager arraignment of the slave classes.

From our perch, we watched as plague upon plague fell upon the Egyptians from Heaven to show them that the God of Abraham, Isaac and Jacob was not One among peers -- but God above all that was worshipped by their society. The point of this whole section of the story, as we pointed out, was God on the move – exposing WHO He is to lost men. We kept asking the nagging question… "How will the whole world know our God?"

The fact is that we find ourselves in this time and place of history in sort of the same place Moses and Aaron did. We are surrounded by men and women who sacrifice all to the pagan gods of fortune, fame, power and pleasure. They do not think there is a God above them beyond the self-made and carefully sculpted gods they have bowed before. They worship money, celebrity, amusement and sexuality. Some barely mask their worship. It is fed by publishing houses, television networks, film makers and entertainment industry specialists the world over. Advertisers appeal to the sensual nature of these who are completely ensnared and often totally oblivious. Standing before the "mass of the powerful" are a few believers who know and love the God that created all things. What's more, we were called to powerfully demonstrate Who this God is before those all about us.

We were not called to JOIN them nor JUDGE them... We were called to REACH them.

We must remember that God has taken the time and energy to expose Who He is and how we can know Him. He began the process in the Garden after man sinned, and expanded the knowledge of Himself over time. Today, we will trace three paths that God wants to establish to Himself: He is at the end of each path drawing men from their darkness into the warmth and light of His presence.

The **first path** is one for the strong follower that needs to be led by a powerful God in the midst of dangers and disappointments.

The **second** is the weak believer that needs to grow strong in his trust of God's plan and direction.

A **third** is the path for the non-believer that needs a relationship with his Creator.

Key Principle: God wants people to know Him – and God wants His people to show Him who He is! God is reaching out to men and women – but they must learn to see Him through the dust the world is kicking up around them!

Go back with me to the story. Before we go too far, take out your Bible and look closely at these names.

Go back to Exodus 6:13 and look at the words: Then the LORD spoke to Moses and to Aaron, and gave them a charge to the sons of Israel and to Pharaoh King of Egypt, to bring the sons of Israel out of the land of Egypt.

Mark the three characters – the so-called three players:

- Moses/Aaron: (the strong believers)
- The Israelites: though at times you will want to place Aaron here! (weak but growing believers)
- The Egyptians and Pharaoh: (unbelievers)

Now turn to *Exodus 7:5* and look at God's purpose in all that He did: *The Egyptians shall know that I am the LORD, when I stretch out My hand on Egypt and bring out the sons of Israel from their midst.*

The one purpose God had in the whole story of the plagues is obvious: The formula: *"that you may know that I am the Lord"* or something similar to it appears eleven times (in Exodus 6:2, 6, 7, 8, 28; 7:5, 17; 8:10, 22; 9:14; and 10:2). Now think through the plagues we read about last time we were together. Did you also notice three patterns? The story offers a way for God to show some important distinctions God makes with people. The biblical truth is that God doesn't see all people in the same way, He does not deal with them in the same way. NO! God distinguishes:

In Plagues 1-3: The Lord distinguishes between his servants, Moses and Aaron, and the servants of the Egyptian gods, the magicians.

- 1st Plague: 7:14-19 Water to blood - Both the Nile and stored water was affected.
- 2nd Plague: 8:1-15 Frogs everywhere!
- 3rd Plague: 8:16-19 Lice, sand flea or chigger infestation

Although the Egyptian magicians duplicate the first two plagues (7:11, 22), they cannot reverse the effects (8:8), and they cannot duplicate the third plague (8:18), finally recognizing "the finger of God" (8:19). In each of these plagues, God acts through Moses and Aaron!

In Plagues 4-6: The Lord distinguished between his people, the Israelites, and the Egyptians.

- 4th Plague: 8:20-32 Flies everywhere!
- 5th Plague: 9:1-7 Death of the livestock.
- 6th Plague: 9:8-12 Boils on the Egyptian people and animals not killed with the livestock.

While the first three plagues affected all of Egypt, the next three don't impact the land of Goshen, where the Israelites live (8:22-23). In the fourth and fifth, God acts directly though Moses prays!

In Plagues 7-9: The Lord distinguished between Himself and everyone else.

- 7th plague: 9:13-35 Hail
- 8th Plague: 10:1-20 Locusts
- 9th Plague: 10:21-29 Plague of darkness

In these plagues, he demonstrates that "there is no one like Me in all the Earth" (9:14); therefore, the severity of the plagues is without precedent (9:18, 9:24, 10:6; 10:14).

In the 10th Plague: The Lord **distinguished Himself** again in this plague. Moses (11:3), the Israelites (11:7) and the Lord (11:6) are all differentiated again.

10th Plague: Death of the Firstborn Children and protected cattle (Exodus 11:1-10)

The Lord executed the 10th plague Himself and not through Moses or Aaron (12:12). Potentially all people could have been affected, but the difference He made was through the instruction of the blood on the door or tent post. This showed clearly that people had the opportunity to be saved from destruction, but they needed to demonstrate faith by obedience to God's Word. Those who didn't were treated very differently from those who did. Even weak believers that obeyed were cared for by God.

This seems like a lot of review, but it is critical to summarize what God showed the people in order for us to see the Biblical point of the story. Careful combining of the ingredients of the text gives us the opportunity to taste extraordinarily of the richness of what God wants us to know. Haphazard observation makes poor spiritual food.

What God said in the ten plagues, as we studied them was this:
You can't trust the daily source of your sustenance of the past (Nile); nor the source of your comfort and personal relief (frogs eating flies). Your superstitions (insects) are worthless and your economy a house of cards (cattle). Your education, health care and technology (magician's boils) can't save you from God's power, nor can you have confidence that your leaders and family (death of first born) will be able to remain strong in the face of the troubles. Resist the God of the Hebrews and suffer! Follow Him and LIVE!

The gods of men are self-made and offer no ultimate rescue. The gods of our culture are NO DIFFERENT than the many gods of the ancient Egyptians. Look at the way our pagan gods fail us today!

- **Riches** fade in the hospital room of the dying.

- **Celebrity** means little when the lights go down and the crowd disperses. This is the reason so many athletes find it nearly impossible to deal with the off season or an injury that takes them from the spotlight.

- **Power** is fleeting. At the dawn of my life, Americans once believed we would have decades of Kennedys in leadership over the country. Two cut down by assassin's bullets, a third marked in scandal, a son crushed in a freak accident – and they were off the stage of leadership.

- The god of **entertainment** and **pleasure** requires an ever-committed legion of followers to pay greater and greater personal costs to stay entertained. Who doesn't know a young person that has fallen into the electronic rabbit hole that eats all his energy and accomplishment in a video game? How many are so busy searching for a friend on Facebook that they cannot develop a single real and touchable human relationship – because they need to keep "channel surfing" for a better and more interesting friend?

Fortune, fame, power and pleasure are the gods made by men. They are hungry for more allegiance—they are insatiable. Sadly, in times of trouble, they offer no rescue. In times of JOY they offer no relationship. They are cold gods – stones shaped by human hands.

From the lessons of the plagues we can grab incredible truths:

Truth 1: God revealed to the strong follower (Moses) that even he needs to be led by a powerful God.

Watch the growth of Moses as he learned to trust God, and you will see a movie about growing mature in the Lord.

- Look where Moses started! Exodus 3 records that when God called him, Moses could ONLY SEE HIMSELF and all his flaws and weaknesses. God reminded him:

Exodus 3:10 "Therefore, come now, and I will send you to Pharaoh, so that you may bring My people, the sons of Israel, out of Egypt." 11 But Moses said to God, "Who am I, that I should go to Pharaoh, and that I should bring the sons of Israel out of Egypt?" 12 And He said, "Certainly I will be with you, and this shall be the sign to you that it is I who have sent you: when you have brought the people out of Egypt, you shall worship God at this mountain."

That is where we begin in our walk with God. He tells us He called us. He offers us a way to walk with Him and have a daily walk with Him. We jerk back, and He shows us that He is ready to walk with us.

Follow Moses forward. Exodus 4 tells of how God walked the weak beginner Moses through seeing His power – a stick comes to life and a hand withers… Moses learned that God isn't unable to accomplish what He calls us to do with Him.

When Moses walked in on Pharaoh in Exodus 5, he had every reason to believe that God's power would push Pharaoh to an immediate response. It did – but not a repentant one. Moses heard the promises of God in the call… but he didn't listen to the problems of the call – the truth was already revealed that Pharaoh would not listen! God said it, but Moses didn't hear it.

Henry Blackaby once wrote: "When God was ready to judge the world with a flood, He came to Noah. When He desired to build a nation for Himself, He turned to Abraham. When He heard His children groaning under Egyptian bondage, He appeared in a burning bush to Moses. They were three of the most ordinary of men but God had work to do, and He knew just who to do it with. God has always given His people assignments that are too big for them to handle alone, so that a watching world can see—not what we can do—but what *God* can do."

Keep following him and you will see Moses growing up in Faith right before your eyes. From the despair of the end of *Exodus 5:22 Then Moses returned to the LORD and said, "O Lord, why have You brought harm to this people? Why did*

You ever send me? 23 Ever since I came to Pharaoh to speak in Your name, he has done harm to this people, and You have not delivered Your people at all," Moses kept moving ahead. God was teaching him to trust.

Follow him through Exodus 6 – 7 – 8 – 9 – 10 – 11 and into 12. Here is what you will read. Time and again "The Lord told Moses to go and speak" and a verse or two later… "And Moses went to Pharaoh and said…" He got it. He learned that God meant what He said. He learned that things looked out of control, but God was sculpting a plan.

Why not just win on the first round? Because God isn't just showing the world Who He is – He is teaching US as well. We need the troubles. We need the defeat… and yes, we need the despair. We need things to be tough to see God's Word in action. We need to be led by a powerful God. Muscles are best seen when things break down and someone strong needs to push!

Truth 2: God revealed to the weaker believer that needs to grow strong in his walk that God was able to work through men to accomplish great things, even when it didn't look like things were going well.

Maybe you don't see yourself as a Moses. Maybe you don't see the strength to move ahead based solely on God's Word. It is good to also note that God's power was not lost on the Israelites; they too learned that God is able and resourceful!

"January 6, 1850, was bitterly cold in Colchester, England, a hard-biting blizzard keeping most worshipers at home. At the Primitive Methodist Chapel on Artillery Street only about a dozen showed up. When it became apparent that even the pastor would not arrive, an unlettered man rose and spoke haltingly from Isaiah 45:22, 'Look unto me, and be ye saved, all the ends of the Earth: for I am God, and there is none else.' Then the crowd dispersed, thinking the day's service a loss—not realizing that a fifteen-year-old boy had ducked into the room to escape the snowstorm, and, hearing the sermon, had been converted. Years later that boy, Charles Haddon Spurgeon, wrote: 'Don't hold back because you cannot preach in St. Paul's; be content to talk to one or two in a cottage. You may cook in small pots as well as in big ones. Little pigeons can carry great messages. Even a little dog can bark at a thief, wake up the master, and save the house.... Do what you do right thoroughly, pray over it heartily, and leave the result to God.'" (*Nelson's Complete Book of Stories, Illustrations and Quotes*)

Truth 3: God revealed Himself to the non-believer that needs a relationship with his Creator.

Pharaoh was an arrogant and stubborn man. He saw himself as the king in his own land, and in his own life! He was used to getting his own way.

Many people come into a religious audience or church congregation in America today just like Pharaoh. It may be why some of you are listening right now. Your problems are buckling your legs, and you are hoping if you do right for an hour, God will back off.

Be careful! Proverbs warns us of the consequences of a hard heart. *Proverbs 29:1 says, He who is often rebuked, and hardens his neck, will suddenly be destroyed, and that without remedy.* That is pretty sobering.

Did you notice that Pharaoh's responses were of a **Hardened Heart**? Such a heart can continue to:

Defy God: The "ignore it and hope it goes away" method. Water to Blood (Exodus 7:23-25):

Exodus7:23 Then Pharaoh turned and went into his house with no concern even for this. ***24*** *So all the Egyptians dug around the Nile for water to drink, for they could not drink of the water of the Nile.* ***25*** *Seven days passed after the LORD had struck the Nile.*

This is a silent way of Defying God! Remember, Pharaoh's initial response was, "Who is the LORD that I should obey his voice?" (Exodus 5:2)

Delay God: "We can obey God tomorrow" method. Frogs (Exodus 8:8-10)

Exodus 8:8 Then Pharaoh called for Moses and Aaron and said, "Entreat the LORD that He remove the frogs from me and from my people; and I will let the people go, that they may sacrifice to the LORD." 9 Moses said to Pharaoh, "The honor is yours to tell me. When shall I entreat for you and your servants and your people, that the frogs be destroyed from you and your houses {that} they may be left only in the Nile?" 10 Then he said, "Tomorrow." So he said, " (May it be) according to your word, that you may know that there is no one like the LORD our God.

So he said, "Tomorrow." In Pharaoh's reactions we see the mistakes that individuals make today when things get difficult in their lives. In times of difficulty, they put God off. He puts off submitting to God until the last possible moment. "Tomorrow," he says. "will be soon enough."

Phil Yancey wrote, "Living in Colorado, I climb mountains. Colorado has 54 mountains rising above 14,000 ft. and every summer I climb some of them. On a summer weekend in the mountains, I see casual hikers who have no idea what they are doing. In sandals, shorts, and T-shirts, carrying a single container of water, they start up a trail at mid-morning. They have no map, no compass, and no rain gear. They also have no apparent knowledge of the lightning storms that roll in many summer afternoons, making it imperative to summit before noon and head for the safety of the timberline (the elevation in a mountainous region above which trees do not grow).

"My neighbor, who volunteers for Alpine Rescue, has told me hair-raising stories of tourists who must be rescued from certain death after wandering off a trail, falling, or simply being exposed to a sudden hailstorm or 30-degree drop in temperature. Nevertheless, regardless of the circumstances, Alpine Rescue always responds to a call for help. Not once have they lectured a hapless tourist, "Well, since you obviously ignored the most basic rules of the wilderness, you'll just have to sit here and bear the consequences. We won't assist you.

"Their mission is rescue, and so they pursue every needy hiker in the wilderness, no matter how undeserving. A whistle, a cry, a flashing mirror, a bonfire, an 'SOS' spelled out in pine branches, a message of distress from a cell phone - any of these signals will cause Alpine Rescue to mobilize teams of medically trained searchers.

"I have come to see the central message of the Bible, too, as one of rescue. In the book of Romans, Paul takes pains to point out that none of us 'deserve' God's mercy and none of us can save ourselves. Like a stranded hiker, all we can do is call for help. A hardened park ranger could look at the efforts of Alpine Rescue as indulging the bad habits of irresponsible tourists. Shouldn't they spend their energy instead handing out rewards to hikers who follow the rules? ('God, I thank you that I am not like other men - robbers, evildoers, adulterers,' prayed the Pharisees.)

"When I posed such a question to my neighbor, she looked at me uncomprehending. 'But our business is rescue!' she said. 'Do you expect us to leave any hiker stranded in the wilderness? I don't care who they are - they need help.' 'In the same way,' said Jesus, 'I tell you, there is rejoicing in the presence of the angels of God over one sinner who repents.'" (Philip Yancey, *Rumors of another World*, pp.154-55)

Deal With God: "I will submit to God on my terms" method. Insects (Exodus 8:24-28)

Exodus 8:24 . And there came great swarms of flies into the house of Pharaoh and the houses of his servants and the land was laid waste because of the swarms of flies in all the land of Egypt. ***25*** *Pharaoh called for Moses and Aaron and said, "Go, sacrifice to your God within the land."* ***26*** *But Moses said, "It is not right to do so, for we will sacrifice to the LORD our God what is an abomination to the Egyptians. If we sacrifice what is an abomination to the Egyptians before their eyes, will they not then stone us?* ***27*** *"We must go a three days' journey into the wilderness and sacrifice to the LORD our God as He commands us."* ***28*** *Pharaoh said, "I will let you go, that you may sacrifice to the LORD your God in the wilderness; only you shall not go very far away. Make supplication for me."*

Pharaoh here offers two different bargains to God and His followers. These proposals strangely parallel **offers that Satan makes a believer today:**

- The first deal we will call the "**Partial Obedience Deal**": You can serve God, but keep one foot in the world (8:25).

- The second deal we will call the **"Partial Commitment Deal"** (8:28): Stay where you can **see** the world (8:28) You can leave, but please "leave with one eye still on Egypt"

Dent without Dedication (9:27-30, 35): The ever popular "convicted without commitment" method. Hail. (Exodus 9:20)

*Exodus 9:20 The one among the servants of Pharaoh who feared the word of the LORD made his servants and his livestock flee into the houses... **27** Then Pharaoh sent for Moses and Aaron, and said to them, " I have sinned this time; the LORD is the righteous one, and I and my people are the wicked ones. **28** Make supplication to the LORD, for there has been enough of God's thunder and hail; and I will let you go, and you shall stay no longer."*

Note that Pharaoh felt bad, but he made no change.

Being convicted of our sins is not the same as being saved from our sins. You can sit in a service with tears streaming down your face because of the deep conviction of your sins, but that does not save you. It takes more than conviction - it take commitment. To be delivered from our sins we must commit ourselves to the Lord.

"You may be in the danger zone ....You have played fast and loose with your life, ignoring warning after warning. You have shoved aside essential truths for so long that your heart has become hardened. And the longer you harden it, the more difficult it will be to allow God's light to finally break through." (Charles Swindoll, *Moses: A Man of Selfless Dedication,* Nashville: Word, 1999, p. 188)

God is reaching out to men and women – but they must learn to see Him through the dust the world is kicking up around them!

Grasping God's Purpose: Lessons in Exodus

Lesson Eleven: Exodus 12:1-28 "The Safe Combination"

It was a huge, dark colored "monstrosity" of a safe. It was also very old. Of all the things stored in the dilapidated shack, this one not only caught my attention… it bothered me. How long had it been where it is now? No one seemed to know. The dust and dirt cried out that it had made a home for itself here many years before. Where did it come from? Again, no one was prepared with an answer. No one knew the story. The owner approached. "Interested in the safe, are you?" "Yes, but I want to know about it first," I replied. "It was in my grandfather's office in Chicago when I was a boy," the old man said. "He got it from his father, who worked on the northwest railroad." "Really", I said. "Have you ever had it opened?" I asked. "No, I have never found anyone who knew how to work the combination lock!" "I don't suppose you are a safe cracker from the old west, are you?" "Sorry", I replied. "Is there any other way to get inside and see what is in there?" I asked. "I am sorry young man," he offered. Then the words that stuck to my heart came out of his mouth. "The safe was designed just like our lives – with one door. The designer knows the combination, and that is the only way the door was made to open. If he were here, he could tell us."

There it was… the truth. Life was made with one exit door by a singular Designer Who knows how to open it, and where the door leads us. Aside from divine interruption, it is the way all of us will leave this life. Our problem isn't understanding the room we are IN now, but knowing where the door leads us. In some ways our exit door from life is more like an elevator than a safe. We will die, and the question is: "Where will we be when we step into the next room?" Fortunately, our Designer didn't leave us without the combination to open the door, nor the information about the destination of the next room. He told us that we can come and be where He is – and that it is a good place. In fact, He told us He wants us to come to Him.

Now comes the problem – He offers only one correct combination to both open the door and to ensure the room we step into is the room He designed for us. Every other combination, carefully made by the turning of the hands of our life will offer the wrong result. We don't get to choose the terms of our final redemption – He alone does. Many have offered Him counsel on what they think He should accept – good deeds accumulated over a long period of life, heroic selfless acts, religious rites and prayers. The truth is, their opinion isn't the one that counts – only the Creator's opinion sets the combination.

Key Principle: God's acceptance is only on God's terms, no one else's opinion really matters!

What did God say about the way to a relationship with Him that would open the door to a relationship in the daily life now and Heaven at death? In the passage selected for this study, He offered us a vivid description of redemption.

Before we go to that description, you should recall what my friends Doug Greenwold and Jim Martin at *Preserving Bible Times* have called the "**Five Storylines of the Bible**." These five help set the stage for the whole of the biblical story of God's Work on Earth. The five are:

- **God** (Who He is, What He cares about)
- **Adversary** (Who he is, How he works)
- **Mutiny** (How it happened and what it caused
- **Fallen Condition** (Why things are broke now), and finally…
- **Redemption** (How God rescues His creation).

Today we will focus on one of the greatest passages in the Bible that offers principles of redemption.

By the time we open to Exodus 12, we find ourselves stepping into the scene of ancient Egypt as the Israelites are leaving bondage as the result of Divine Intervention. The scene is a redemption one – a motif of salvation. God offered us a window view of "Seven Principles of Redemption" in this lesson.

Before we examine them, we should address a basic question. Is this really an important subject to God? It is obviously important to us…

we need the combination to open the lock that opens the door to the room prepared for us. That isn't the question. The question is: "Is this important to God?" We can confidently offer an answer: "Yes!" because He made a memorial for the occasion:

Memorial - The way of redemption should be remembered:

Exodus 12:14 "Now this day will be a memorial to you, and you shall celebrate it as a feast to the LORD; throughout your generations you are to celebrate it as a permanent ordinance. 24 And you shall observe this event as an ordinance for you and your children forever. 25 When you enter the land which the LORD will give you, as He has promised, you shall observe this rite. 26 And when your children say to you, 'What does this rite mean to you?' 27 you shall say, 'It is a Passover sacrifice to the LORD Who passed over the houses of the sons of Israel in Egypt when He smote the Egyptians, but spared our homes.'" And the people bowed low and worshiped. 28 Then the sons of Israel went and did so; just as the LORD had commanded Moses and Aaron, so they did.

God made a "holiday" for the purpose of commemorating the act of redemption from Egypt. He called it a permanent ordinance (12:14) – even using the term forever (12:24). The Jewish people were never to stop recalling this day! Entry to the land was not a reason to stop (12:25), as it was to be a sign for their generations to come (12:26-28).

The memory was so important that God prescribed how He wanted the celebration to work. He wanted the memorial to include a cessation of labor, a change of diet, and – at least for the first one – a symbolic act of obedience that went contrary to everything the people knew.

Look at the three ways the memorial was to be observed:

No Work:

Exodus 12: 16 On the first day you shall have a holy assembly, and another holy assembly on the seventh day; no work at all shall be done on them, except what must be eaten by every person, that alone may be prepared by you. 17 You shall also observe the Feast of Unleavened Bread, for on this very day I brought your hosts out of the land of Egypt; therefore, you shall observe this day throughout your generations as a permanent ordinance.

God wanted special times to be set aside by removing the temptation to be distracted by ordinary life. It was to be different from the norm. It was to be about the memory and the relationship with God, not advancing one's career. It bears remembering in a modern church environment where we often use the church for networking and fundraising – money and work are fine – but they can distract us from our purpose in growing our walk with God. Jesus made that argument with a whip in the Temple long ago… we need to be careful about our pursuits as we grow our love for God.

Diet Limitations:

Exodus 12:18 In the first month, on the fourteenth day of the month at evening, you shall eat unleavened bread... 19 Seven days there shall be no leaven found in your houses; for whoever eats what is leavened, that person shall be cut off from the congregation of Israel, whether he is an alien or a native of the land. 20 You shall not eat anything leavened; in all your dwellings you shall eat unleavened bread.

God picked out something common to everyone – bread. It was the symbol of the "needs of man" as demonstrated much later in the prayer by Jesus: *Give us this day our daily bread.* Here God commanded that they eat a different kind of bread. It provided both memory and connection to the event. It also separated the observers from those who felt obedience was optional. It is essential that we understand that God is concerned with what goes IN to the observance and worship times we have. He gets to specify what comprises acceptable celebration and worship.

Symbolic Practices:

Exodus 12:21 Then Moses called for all the elders of Israel and said to them, "Go and take for yourselves lambs according to your families, and slay the Passover lamb. 22

You shall take a bunch of hyssop and dip it in the blood which is in the basin, and apply some of the blood that is in the basin to the lintel and the two door-posts; and none of you shall go outside the door of his house until morning. 23 For the LORD will pass through to smite the Egyptians; and when He sees the blood on the lintel and on the two doorposts, the LORD will pass over the door and will not allow the destroyer to come in to your houses to smite you."

Obviously, God told them to do this only on the initial observance, and that will lead us right into our subject. With the idea firmly planted that this is an important day to the Creator, let's take a brief look at the rest of Exodus 12 and see if the principles of redemption are clear.

Seven Principles of Redemption:

Principle One: Redemption is about offering a new start to life. (Life begins at redemption.)

Exodus12:1 Now the LORD said to Moses and Aaron in the land of Egypt, 2 "This month shall be the beginning of months for you; it is to be the first month of the year to you."

The Bible uses terms of "newness" when it describes one who begins to walk in a deliberate subservient relationship to God:

2 Corinthians 5:17 Therefore if anyone is in Christ, he is a new creature; the old things passed away; behold, new things have come.

"The phrase '*a new creature*' (καινὴ κτίσις kainē ktisis) occurs also in *Galatians 6:15*. The word rendered "creature" (κτίσις ktisis) means properly in the New Testament, creation." (*Barnes Commentary*)

The Bible explains that man was created to have a relationship with God. When that relationship was severed because of mutiny – God created a redemption that would allow man to be "newly created." In the Exodus story, that newness was given ceremony in the inauguration of the calendar!

Principle Two: Redemption comes from making obedience a personal decision. (It is a personal and individual act.)

Exodus 12:3 "Speak to all the congregation of Israel, saying, 'On the tenth of this month they are each one to take a lamb for themselves, according to their fathers' households, a lamb for each household.' 4 Now if the household is too small for a lamb, then he and his neighbor nearest to his house are to take one according to the number of persons in them; according to what each man should eat, you are to divide the lamb. 5 Your lamb shall be an unblemished male a year old; you may take it from the sheep or from the goats…."

Exodus 12:21 Then Moses called for all the elders of Israel and said to them, "Go and take for yourselves lambs according to your families, and slay the Passover lamb. 22 You shall take a bunch of hyssop and dip it in the blood which is in the basin, and apply some of the blood that is in the basin to the lintel and the two doorposts; and none of you shall go outside the door of his house until morning. 23 For the LORD will pass through to smite the Egyptians; and when He sees the blood on the lintel and on the two doorposts, the LORD will pass over the door and will not allow the destroyer to come in to your houses to smite you."

God wanted each generation of Israelites to understand that individual belief, and individual use of the blood would be necessary to be saved.

Exodus 12:3-5 gave careful instructions about the preparation of the home before the Lord executed judgment on the Egyptian firstborn. Each man was instructed to take "A LAMB" (12:3) for his house. If "THE LAMB" (12:4) was too much for the small household, the man was to share with his neighbor and not waste. The lamb was to be spotless, and sacrificed that its blood may be used as a marker. It was to be killed and personally applied as "YOUR LAMB" (12:5). The message for the children of Israel was compelling: they needed to act personally believe the message of God, and follow the direction of God to be saved from calamity and set free from bondage. Tonight, chicken was not on the menu!

Principle Three: Redemption comes from a blood payment. (Blood was the necessary payment.)

Exodus 12:6 You shall keep it until the fourteenth day of the same month, then the whole assembly of the congregation of Israel is to kill it at twilight. 7 Moreover, they shall take some of the blood and put it on the two doorposts and on the lintel of the houses in which they eat it....

Exodus 12:13 The blood shall be a sign for you on the houses where you live; and when I see the blood I will pass over you, and no plague will befall you to destroy you when I strike the land of Egypt.

It was God's instruction that the first holy festival be an observance that would clearly mark a believer from the unbelieving world in which he lives. After generations of serving Egyptian Pharaohs, the cries of the children of Israel went up before the Lord God, and He sent a deliverer to release his captive children. Exodus 12 records that the power of God would strike down the firstborn of every home in Egypt not protected by the mark of lamb's blood on the door or tent post. The God of Abraham proved too powerful for the mighty Pharaoh of Egypt. The purchasing of the freedom of God's people was forever to be symbolized by the Passover feast.

The instruction given by God to Moses was to be continually observed. A close look at God's instruction yields the clear principle He wanted each generation to understand...Individuals would have to *use* the blood. Individuals would then have to wait and trust that God would keep His word. They would have to silently wait and trust that the blood was enough to protect them from the judgment of God.

God has always told His people to be careful about blood.

When God cursed Cain for killing Able, He told Cain that Able's blood cried out from the ground – making it sound alive (Gen 4).

When God told Noah what he and his sons could eat, He specified not to "ingest blood," calling it "the life of another" (Gen. 9).

In the Law, God told Moses to warn the people, *For as for the life of all flesh, its blood is identified with its life. Therefore I said to the sons of Israel, 'You are not to eat the blood of any flesh, for the life of all flesh is its blood; whoever eats it shall be cut off' (Leviticus 17:14).*

The Levitical system of sacrifice offered much about killing and blood. Later, the writer of Hebrews summarized the whole package saying, *And according to the Law, one may almost say, all things are cleansed with blood, and without shedding of blood there is no forgiveness (Heb. 9:22).*

Blood is symbolically important to God. Drinking blood was forbidden. Spilling blood for fun – off limits. Is it any wonder that our anti-biblical culture is saturated in Hollywood blood pictures? Is it surprising how so many spend much of the week in digital murder? Does a vampire craze make sense in a reactionary anti-biblical culture? Sure it does.

The sad part is that so many believers don't get why this is important. Our salvation was accomplished in blood – and no other way.

John instructs us in *1 John 1:7 But if we walk in the Light as He Himself is in the Light, we have fellowship with one another, and the blood of Jesus His Son cleanses us from all sin.*

Principle Four: Redemption comes from intimate action. (You become "one" with the Redeemer!")

Exodus 12:8: They shall eat the flesh that same night, roasted with fire, and they shall eat it with unleavened bread and bitter herbs.

Just as the commemoration had to do with the denial of some food: *(Unleavened bread shall be eaten throughout the seven days; and nothing leavened shall be seen among you, nor shall any leaven be seen among you in all your borders (Exodus13:7),* it also became part of the plan to ingest the animal of sacrifice as a picture of accepting the sacrifice as their Redeemer. They ate it because they were told to eat it. Killing a part of their flock was not done without reservation. Add to that, no left-overs were allowed. This was a single meal, and the cost was significant! Why order such a thing? The symbol was essential to teach the truth about the intimate joining of the Redeemer to the redeemed.

A real believer would need to allow the Redeemer inside of them.

That is the message we still preach. You cannot be saved by simply observing Jesus. It is a volitional choice and an intimate act of thankful surrender to the One Who gave His all for us.

1 Peter 1:18 For you know that it was not with perishable things such as silver or gold that you were redeemed from the empty way of life handed down to you from your forefathers, but with precious blood, as of a lamb unblemished and spotless, the blood of Christ.

Principle Five: Redemption is bounded in following God's instructions. (You can't decide something else will satisfy Him.)

Exodus 12:9 Do not eat any of it raw or boiled at all with water, but rather roasted with fire, both its head and its legs along with its entrails. 10 And you shall not leave any of it over until morning, but whatever is left of it until morning, you shall burn with fire.

This isn't deep. Just look at God's language. He isn't offering suggestions. He knows what He desires, and He doesn't throw it open to discussion. The text is exacting – because that is how God is. We don't decide what He wants – the combination lock was designed by Him.

Principle Six: Redemption begins a journey to a new life. (Get ready for what comes after…)

Exodus 12:11 Now you shall eat it in this manner: with your loins girded, your sandals on your feet, and your staff in your hand; and you shall eat it in haste—it is the LORD'S Passover.

I LOVE this part! It is as though God is saying, "Hang on boys! You are all just getting started on a new journey!"

That was true at my redemption as well. When I first invited Jesus in my heart, my new life engaged. My old sloppy way of thinking had to be systematically reset by God's Word and God's Spirit. My habits needed a change, my mind a scrub, my life an adjustment…

Principle Seven: Redemption rejected is judgment invited. (We must choose to accept the conditions as God laid them down.)

Exodus 12:12 For I will go through the land of Egypt on that night, and will strike down all the firstborn in the land of Egypt, both man and beast; and against all the gods of Egypt I will execute judgments—I am the LORD.

It is worth noting that God warned them all and gave them all a way of escape. One of the brutal facts of redemption is that we don't get to make our own rules! If we choose to ignore God's Word, the end is certain for us.

"It is gratitude that prompted an old man to visit an old broken pier on the eastern seacoast of Florida. Every Friday night, until his death in 1973, he would return, walking slowly and slightly stooped with a large bucket of shrimp. The sea gulls would flock to this old man, and he would feed them from his bucket. Many years before, in October, 1942, Captain Eddie Rickenbacker was on a mission in a B-17 to deliver an important message to General Douglas MacArthur in New Guinea. But there was an unexpected detour which would hurl Captain Eddie into the most harrowing adventure of his life.

"Somewhere over the South Pacific the *Flying Fortress* became lost beyond the reach of radio. Fuel ran dangerously low, so the men ditched their plane in the ocean. For nearly a month Captain Eddie and his companions would fight the water, and the weather, and the scorching sun. They spent many sleepless nights recoiling as giant sharks rammed their rafts. The largest raft was nine by five. The biggest shark, .ten feet long.

“But of all their enemies at sea, one proved most formidable: starvation. Eight days out, their rations were long gone or destroyed by the salt water. It would take a miracle to sustain them. And a miracle occurred. In Captain Eddie's own words, "Cherry," that was the B- 17 pilot, Captain William Cherry, "read the service that afternoon, and we finished with a prayer for deliverance and a hymn of praise. There was some talk, but it tapered off in the oppressive heat. With my hat pulled down over my eyes to keep out some of the glare, I dozed off."

“Now this is still Captain Rickenbacker talking, "Something landed on my head. I knew that it was a sea gull. I don't know how I knew, I just knew. Everyone else knew too. No one said a word, but peering out from under my hat brim without moving my head, I could see the expression on their faces. They were staring at that gull. The gull meant food if I could catch it." And the rest, as they say, is history

.

Captain Eddie caught the gull. Its flesh was eaten. Its intestines were used for bait to catch fish. The survivors were sustained and their hopes renewed because a lone sea gull, uncharacteristically hundreds of miles from land, offered itself as a sacrifice. You know that Captain Eddie made it. And now you also know.that he never forgot. Because every Friday evening, about sunset, on a lonely stretch along the eastern Florida seacoast, .you could see an old man walking slightly bent; white-haired, bushy-eye-browed. His bucket filled with shrimp was to feed the gulls.to remember that one, which, on a day long past, gave itself without a struggle, like manna in the wilderness. “ (Excerpted From: *The Old Man and the Gulls,* from Paul Harvey's *The Rest of the Story* by Paul Aurandt, 1977, quoted in *Heaven Bound Living*, Knofel Stanton, Standard, 1989, p. 79-80)

The men used the life of the gull to keep them alive, just as we take the blood of Jesus to give us life. God has made a way of redemption, but we must heed His conditions!

Grasping God's Purpose: Lessons in Exodus

Lesson Twelve: Exodus 13:1-21 "Take the Long Road Home"

I confess that I am not always a patient man. I like short cuts – but they must be proven. I only notice the flowers along the drive because God gave me a wife to call them to my attention. I read management and efficiency literature. Things that are poorly managed bug me. Perhaps that is why this passage put a "burr under my saddle." In these days of efficiency management, God's way of doing things can grate us the wrong way. He can take the long way around things and make a point in what seems an inefficient way. This study will help us understand and relate to the "indirect God" and appreciate the brilliance of His method of teaching!

In the text for our study, there are two clear parts: God makes commands (12:43-13:16) and then begins an example leading the people (13:17-22). The two sections have one thing in common: both are inefficient in their execution. Why doesn't God do things the short and easy way? Let's take the passage apart and it will become clearer. While we do, there is a principle that we will learn:

Key Principle: God knows the short way is not always the best way to move us ahead. He takes His time to make sure the way we head is pleasing to Him!

The Commands(12:43-13:16)

Timing of the Commands (Ex. 12:43)

Look at the opening Command in *Exodus 12:43 The LORD said to Moses and Aaron, "This is the ordinance of the Passover: no foreigner is to eat of it…"*

Something strikes me strangely about these words… Before we explore what God commanded Moses, I had a question… why offer detailed instructions before you get the people moving out of Pharaoh's way? Bear in mind the passage is set while they are still in Egypt. It can be as simple as the idea that the record was expanded by Moses later. There is no reason to believe he wrote the final form of what we have that night. At the same time, it occurs to me that there are perhaps two spiritual and yet incredibly practical reasons why this was placed where it is in the story:

First: They were not ready to have God lead them anywhere until they were ready to listen! (and neither are we!) I have met many believers who have labored over God's will for some venture or question. Have you ever been fasting and praying and still not hearing clearly from God while you are in the will and the way of God—about what He wants you to do, or where He wants you to go with your issue? It is worth noting that if you are not walking in the will of God you will need to understand that God seldom raises His voice. His Words soak into your ears by a whisper…not a scream.

If you are not close enough to God to hear Him whisper, then you may find yourself wandering continuously with no idea where you are headed…because God's whisper is only for those that are close enough, and those that are quiet enough to listen. It is as if God says: "If you're really interested in hearing me, move everything: every obstacle, every encumbrance, everything that distracts you from Me out of the way." While God had the attention of Israel on the miracle of the Passover – perhaps He used their short attention span to speak words that would last for all their generations. I suspect there is another reason God spoke before He moved the people out.

Second, God was not ready to show His power until they were ready to proclaim His right of ownership! God strips a believer of personal ownership before He shows what belonging to Him means. Have you noticed how God speaks in Scripture as though He is in charge? The writer of a series of billboards seems to "get it" in the *God Speaks* series in the DFW area:

The billboards are a simple black background with white text. No fine print or sponsoring organization is included. The sponsorship for these "God Speaks" billboards is anonymous:

"Let's meet at my house Sunday before the game." – God
"C'mon over and bring the kids." – God
"What part of "Thou Shalt Not didn't you understand?" – God
"We need to talk." – God
"Keep using my name in vain, I'll make rush hour longer." – God
"Loved the wedding, invite me to the marriage." – God
"That 'Love Thy Neighbor' thing, I meant it." – God
"I love you and you and you and you and. "– God
"Will the road you're on get you to my place?" – God
"Follow me." –God
"Big bang theory, you've got to be kidding." – God
"My way is the highway." – God
"Need directions?" – God
"You think it's hot here?" – God
"Have you read my #1 best seller? There will be a test." – God
"Do you have any idea where you're going?" – God
And finally: "Don't make me come down there." – God

I am not being snide, but it isn't in the nature of man to submit to rules or even the concept of Divine ownership. Our pride is big and our resistance is significant – even when God moves into our lives in a PROFOUND WAY, like He did on the first Passover.

Substance of the Commands - Four Types: Ex. 12:43–13:16)

Type One: The Distinction Commands (Ex. 12:43-51)

Exodus 12:43 The LORD said to Moses and Aaron, "This is
the ordinance of the Passover: no foreigner is to eat of it. 44
but every man's slave purchased with money, after you have
circumcised him, then he may eat of it. 45 A sojourner or a
hired servant shall not eat of it. 4 It is to be eaten in a
single house; you are not to bring forth any of the flesh
outside of the house, nor are you to break any bone of it. 47
All the congregation of Israel are to celebrate this. 48 But if
a stranger sojourns with you, and celebrates the Passover to
the LORD, let all his males be circumcised, and then let him
come near to celebrate it; and he shall be like a native of the
land. But no uncircumcised person may eat of it. 49 The

same law shall apply to the native as to the stranger who sojourns among you." 50 Then all the sons of Israel did so; they did just as the LORD had commanded Moses and Aaron. 51 And on that same day the LORD brought the sons of Israel out of the land of Egypt by their hosts.

God said essentially: "*Set apart this feast of the Passover and include only those I have specified to observe it for your generations!*" (12:43-51). God has a new and special identity for people who desire to walk through the wilderness with Him. It is a distinct people, with a unique set of markers and a unique set of standards. Failure to come under His Word bars you from participation! Three important lessons can be seen here:

First, we need to include who God includes, and exclude who God excludes. In the "tolerance at any cost" laden generation, we need to remember that throwing in the towel on God's standards so that we can be loving and accepting of everyone is NOT a marker of godliness; it is a warped version of truth. We need to be gracious and loving as God's people. At the same time, that grace stops at the edge of God's Word. We must be careful, for all around us are voices that call us to allow things God said we cannot allow – and call it all LOVE.

Second, we need to serve an eviction notice on a lot of stuff left over from our old life. That principle can be even more closely applied to my own life. Anything that doesn't please God and doesn't honor God needs to be shown the door. Things that are hindering your being properly aligned with the Spirit of God must fall under His Word on the subject. You can't bring in the treasure until you take the trash out. God doesn't bless a mess – in ministry or in heart. Once we've evicted every encumbrance—then God will move in our heart with free course. Don't argue to hold on to encumbrances out of some warped theological theory – just give them up.

Third, on a more positive note**, careful observation of the text about the meal reveals that God was signaling a family relationship in the observance**. Those who are a part of the family are to take part ***as sons*** (12:42). God's work in people started through the family, and He illustrates the relationship as that of a son. Interesting, in the time this was a title of a young man that respected his father, and wanted to be identified as part of his legacy. How the enemy has launched an attack on this part of the identity!

Those who are not part of the family are not to take part unless they have been circumcised as the family (12:43-45, 48-49). The people were to be examined and to join the people of God by submitting themselves to reverence one of God's " more difficult to follow commands." Being a part of God's program was not a negotiation, nor did people come in with a list of demands. It was a privilege to be a part of God's family. God's provision was a family experience and cannot be shared outside the house (12:46).

Those who refused to join God's family failed to receive the benefits of the family. It isn't a right; it is a privilege to have God's blessings! The off-ramp of Hell highway is available, but you must turn the vehicle! Everyone in the family is to participate – it is not left to your choice (12:47). If you are a part of God's program, then you do what God says to do. He isn't taking a headcount on what we think; He's telling us His expectation. After they committed to follow the Lord, they were commanded to move ahead (12:50-51). That's the pattern of the Bible: trust, then obey, then get blessed. God has no grandchildren and every one must make a decision of whether to trust God or not on their own.

Type Two: The Devotion Commands (Ex. 13:1-2)

Exodus 13:1 Then the LORD spoke to Moses, saying, 2 "Sanctify to Me every firstborn, the first offspring of every womb among the sons of Israel, both of man and beast; it belongs to Me."

"Set apart (Devote) the first born of man and beast – they are MINE" (13:1). God knew that His purchase made in Egypt long ago would quickly be forgotten when the people were redeemed and out of the harsh bondage.

Believers tend to lose their enthusiasm the further they get from their lost life. God told them to recall the beginning story with every new generation! Obviously, the tendency of believers both then and now is to be cheap and cheat God on His property!

The roof of the church hall of a little Swiss church, at the turn of the 20th century, was falling down. So the members of the church held regular prayer meetings in the hall after the service to pray for funds to repair the roof. There was an old man, known to be very tight with his money, who used to attend and sit near the back of the hall. He could sneak out just before the collection plate came round at the end of the prayer meeting. One Sunday, he was held up on his way to the prayer meeting in the Hall by the vicar and could only find a seat at the front of the church. During the prayer meeting, a piece of the roof fell and hit him on the head. Feeling spoken to by the Lord, he stood up and said "Lord, I'll give $1000." A voice at the back of the church was heard to say, "Hit him again, Lord!"

God wanted the first - of everything. He bought them and paid for all of them, but He wanted them to remember! Later on the price for redemption of a human first-born male was set at 5 shekels (Numbers 18:16). Moses in turn gave the people the same two great commands:

Type Three: The Memorial Commands (Ex. 13:3-10)

Exodus 13:3 Moses said to the people, "Remember this day in which you went out from Egypt, from the house of slavery; for by a powerful hand the LORD brought you out from this place. And nothing leavened shall be eaten. 4 On this day in the month of Abib, you are about to go forth. 5 It shall be when the LORD brings you to the land of the Canaanite, the Hittite, the Amorite, the Hivite and the Jebusite, which He swore to your fathers to give you, a land flowing with milk and honey, that you shall observe this rite in this month. 6 For seven days you shall eat unleavened bread, and on the seventh day there shall be a feast to the LORD. 7 Unleavened bread shall be eaten throughout the seven days; and nothing leavened shall be seen among you, nor shall any leaven be seen among you in all your borders. 8 You shall tell your son on that day, saying, 'It is because of what the LORD did for me when I came out of Egypt.' 9 And it shall serve as a sign to you on your hand, and as a reminder on your forehead, that the law of the LORD may be in your mouth; for with a powerful hand the LORD brought you out of Egypt. 10 Therefore, you shall keep this ordinance at its appointed time from year to year."

The short read is this: "Memorialize our deliverance in this week-long festival! Do so by getting leaven out of the feast for a week, eating unleavened bread each year at this time!" (13:3-10).

The "memorial commands" are these:

- The memory of the powerful work of God would be seen in a meal (13:3a). This theme isn't new to the Bible. There was a meal covenant in Scripture that was shared when peace was forged between warring parties (Psalm 23, Jacob and Laban in Genesis).

- Leaven was natural, unleavened bread was rushed and unnatural. It went against the grain (13:3b). It was faster to make, but harder to swallow. In many ways, God's command was to make people reverse the normal ways they did things to recall the events of the wilderness.

- God was deeply interested in the timing of the event (13:4) and the continued observance of the event (13:5-7). He wanted them to concentrate all their effort on even cleaning any of the "leaven" they had in the camp, carefully cleaning it out! (13:7b)

Notice how many times he says "with a strong hand." The Hebrew root of this word is: khaw-zak' which means "to fasten on to" "to bind." The pun was this: just as God delivered you by "binding you" to His hand, so this observance shall bind you to Him!

Don't be so quick to think that God doesn't care about observances. I want to challenge that idea. I know that we can come dressed however we want and God can hear us. I know that we can lie in a hammock and worship God in a small Bible study at home with our friends. I know that there are no biblical commands to erect buildings as churches. I know the job description of clergy is very much more about character in Timothy and Titus – than about what they do. Yet, I do not conclude that being a part of a living body of a local church is unimportant. I do dress to be here. I do want to worship corporately….and I do see a God in Scripture Who cares about observances – how they are done, what is included in the services, and who should participate.

Let's not keep settling for the downward tug of our times to make everything into a barnyard dance or rock concert. God cares what we do, when we do it, how we are inside and outside. Apply that as the Spirit leads, but don't dismiss it. Two guys at Dunkin Donuts talking about Jesus with no accountability or leadership structure is NOT a local church - even if modern writers say it is.

Type Four: The Devotion Commands (Ex. 13:11-16)

Exodus 13:11 Now when the LORD brings you to the land of the Canaanite, as He swore to you and to your fathers, and gives it to you, 12 you shall devote to the LORD the first offspring of every womb, and the first offspring of every beast that you own; the males belong to the LORD. 13 But every first offspring of a donkey you shall redeem with a lamb, but if you do not redeem it, then you shall break its neck; and every firstborn of man among your sons you shall redeem. 14 And it shall be when your son asks you in time to come, saying, 'What is this?' then you shall say to him, 'With a powerful hand the LORD brought us out of Egypt, from the house of slavery. 15 It came about, when Pharaoh was stubborn about letting us go, that the LORD killed every firstborn in the land of Egypt, both the firstborn of man and the firstborn of beast. Therefore, I sacrifice to the LORD the males, the first offspring of every womb, but every firstborn of my sons I redeem.' 16 So it shall serve as a sign on your hand and as phylacteries on your forehead, for with a powerful hand the LORD brought us out of Egypt.

A quick read on this section may be: "Devote the first born of our children and our animals to the Lord remembering that they are the purchase price of our redemption from slavery!" (13:11-16).
I think it is worth remembering that, **"Everyone is prepared to sacrifice someone else's stuff, but not his own!**"

A mother was preparing pancakes for her sons, Kevin who is 5, and Ryan who is 3. The boys began to argue over who would get the first pancake. Their mother saw the opportunity for a moral lesson so she said: "If Jesus were sitting here, He would say, 'Let my brother have the first pancake. I can wait." Kevin turned to his younger brother and said, "*Hey Ryan, you be Jesus*."

God told the people to offer back to Him the first born of their children, not by taking their lives, but by a sacrifice of a lamb (13:11-13). God kept this command Himself! Ironic that this would be the time when God's very own firstborn son would become the "Lamb slain" to purchase men! God has people give to help them recall who really owns what we have:
Have you ever noticed how big $100.00 looks when you take it to church, yet how small it looks when you take it to the mall?

Don't skip Exodus 13:13. The donkey was unclean so they couldn't sacrifice it - so they used a lamb instead. If someone could not sacrifice a lamb, then the donkey's neck would be broken. It was either redeemed, or it was DEAD – no middle ground. That's a lesson in the judicial nature of a Holy God.

In our passage, God made commands (13:1-16) and then offered an example (13:17-22) leading the people. Quickly look at the example God gave…

The example of Leadership (Ex. 13:17-20)

The commands now given, God led the people out. Look at what the example teaches us:

Protection: God protects us from *US*:

God led them the long way to help them overcome a fear He knew they would have (13:17).

Exodus 13:17 Now when Pharaoh had let the people go, God did not lead them by the way of the land of the Philistines, even though it was near; for God said, "The people might change their minds when they see war, and return to Egypt."

The route chosen by God was southeast towards Sinai. Why? To avoid possible militaristic confrontation with the Egyptians. Because that would encourage people with shallow minds and tunnel vision to go back. Sometime we should thank God not just for His faithfulness in what we went through—but the trouble that we avoided because He shielded us. We may just need to thank God for what we missed along the way…instead of just thanking God for what He brought you out through.

Organization: God gave them a chance to spread out and get organized before the journey began (13:18).

Exodus 13:18 Hence God led the people around by the way of the wilderness to the Red Sea; and the sons of Israel went up in martial array from the land of Egypt.

They needed a chance to get in ranks before they underwent *attacks*, and God gave them the time and space.

Opportunity: God gave them the time necessary to keep their promises.

If they had to ***run***, they couldn't take the bones of their fathers as they promised! (13:19)

Exodus 13:19 Moses took the bones of Joseph with him, for he had made the sons of Israel solemnly swear, saying, "God will surely take care of you, and you shall carry my bones from here with you."

Preparation: God gave them a glimpse of the journey before they got into the wilderness (Note Exodus 13:20).

Exodus 13:20 Then they set out from Succoth and camped in Etham on the edge of the wilderness.

Direction: God gave them direction – clear and distinct.

Exodus 3:21 The LORD was going before them in a pillar of cloud by day to lead them on the way, and in a pillar of fire by night to give them light, that they might travel by day and by night. 22 He did not take away the pillar of cloud by day, nor the pillar of fire by night, from before the people.

Why doesn't God do things the short and easy way? Because He knows the shortcut isn't the best way to get what you need from the journey! He takes His time to make sure the WAY we head is pleasing to Him!

Grasping God's Purpose: Lessons in Exodus

Lesson Thirteen: Exodus 14:1-31 "A Choice Vessel"

Walking through Colonial Williamsburg, I **was struck by the *simplicity* of the vessels** that our forefathers used to care for their needs. The days of molded plastic and cheaply machined glass have certainly made a change in the quality and stylishness of even our simplest drinking cups! One thought was particularly clear, it wasn't the beauty of the vessel that made it valuable, it was the usability of the vessel. The most beautifully carved bucket was only worth having if it was water tight. In the same way, though God wants to use me as a vessel that will bring honor to Him, it is only possible if I make choices that open up His use of me.

What choices can I make that will open myself to being used by Him?

Key Principle: To become a vessel God can use, I must understand and then live the choices that God will be honored by.

Some of our problems stem from a lack of knowledge, but most of them stem from simple willful disobedience. Exodus 14 offers at least Ten Choices that I can make to become a useable vessel to God! Each of the ten must be grasped, but are only effective when put into action:

The Ten Choices of a Vessel fit for Use:

Choose to recognize that God has the right to use me to reach others even by taking me through difficult and trying times. (14:1-4).

Exodus 14:1 Now the LORD spoke to Moses, saying, 2 "Tell the sons of Israel to turn back and camp before Pi-hahiroth, between Migdol and the sea; you shall camp in front of Baal-zephon, opposite it, by the sea. 3 For Pharaoh will say of the sons of Israel, 'They are wandering aimlessly in the land; the wilderness has shut them in.' 4 "Thus I will harden Pharaoh's heart, and he will chase after them; and I will be honored through Pharaoh and all his army, and the Egyptians will know that I am the LORD." And they did so.

God's plan for Israel was not going to be an easy one, but that was the one Moses was to obey, announce and lead. Moses was in the difficult predicament of sharing unpopular truth. Believers should get used to it – truth is often inconvenient, but always helpful!

I liked this: "Have you ever found yourself in a predicament? We have a lot of word pictures in the English language to describe being in a predicament. We hear phrases such as 'you sure have painted yourself into a corner,' of being 'caught between a rock and a hard place,' being 'up against the wall' or 'in a pickle.' A least one person has defined a predicament as being, 'A lawyer who specializes in suing doctors for medical malpractice and finding himself in need of major surgery.'" (Charles Swindoll. *Moses: A Man of Selfless Devotion*, Nashville: Word Publishing, 1999. p. 211)

The events of our lives are not random, God has crafted a time and place for us. We forget that when things go wrong. More often than not, we wonder if we have deserved some spanking when things don't go our way. In the face of stern difficulty, we even convince ourselves that the reason we are going through trouble is something we have done. It seldom occurs to us that the wilderness and the Sea of Reeds is part of the call of God for us. God has a plan for the troubles!

In the text, note that God had several reasons for the journey direction of Moses. First, God wanted to lure in Pharaoh. Sometimes God uses our lives to pull in the lives of godless men. It is exciting when that purpose is to soften their hearts to see His love and goodness – but that wasn't the case here. God used the testimony of the people of God, and Moses their leader, to bring a hardness into him that would set him up for judgment. As uncomfortable as that could have been for any of us – our lives are about recognizing God's right to use us for His purposes.

The ultimate end point of God's plan was what it always is: to expose who He is to man and to the heavenly host. That is His big plan, and we have the opportunity to be used by Him today to do it! For this reason, Paul reminded the Corinthians:

2 Corinthians 2:14 But thanks be to God, who always leads us in triumph in Christ, and manifests through us the sweet aroma of the knowledge of Him in every place. 15 For we are a fragrance of Christ to God among those who are being saved and among those who are perishing; 16 to the one an aroma from death to death, to the other an aroma from life to life. And who is adequate for these things? 17 For we are not like many, peddling the word of God, but as from sincerity, but as from God, we speak in Christ in the sight of God.

Do you believe that God has the unreserved right to use your life for any purpose that will fit His plan – even if that use doesn't fit YOUR plan? Moses had to believe that, or he would have been utterly ineffective as God's leader and spokesman – and so will we.

Choose to remember that power is not often where it appears to be in a fallen world. God allowed Pharaoh to feel a sense of control and power that was not there! (14:5-9).

Exodus 14:5 When the king of Egypt was told that the people had fled, Pharaoh and his servants had a change of heart toward the people, and they said, "What is this we have done, that we have let Israel go from serving us?" 6 So he made his chariot ready and took his people with him; 7 and he took six hundred select chariots, and all the other chariots of Egypt with officers over all of them. 8 The LORD hardened the heart of Pharaoh, king of Egypt, and he chased after the sons of Israel as the sons of Israel were going out boldly. 9 Then the Egyptians chased after them with all the horses and chariots of Pharaoh, his horsemen and his army, and they overtook them camping by the sea, beside Pi-hahiroth, in front of Baal-zephon.

The human view was a powerful Pharaoh and a puny Moses – an organized army and a hapless camp of clueless slaves. That IS the human view – but it is NOT the truth! God was there. His power moved men, and soon would move seas, mountains and monuments. God can and will shake the foundations when it suits His purposes! Towering countries will be brought low for His purposes. Famous men and women will be swept aside by the tide of His story. Power is not where it appears to be!

Choose to accept sometimes even friends and even God's people won't understand what God is doing in your life - and why! (14:10).

Rather, **expect that people will look for someone to blame** when they are hurt and cannot understand their pain. Accept the fact that they are wrong in what they are saying, but **deal with them patiently**! (14:11-12).

Exodus 14:10 As Pharaoh drew near, the sons of Israel looked, and behold, the Egyptians were marching after them, and they became very frightened; so the sons of Israel cried out to the LORD. 11 Then they said to Moses, "Is it because there were no graves in Egypt that you have taken us away to die in the wilderness? Why have you dealt with us in this way, bringing us out of Egypt? 12 Is this not the word that we spoke to you in Egypt, saying, 'Leave us alone that we may serve the Egyptians'? For it would have been better for us to serve the Egyptians than to die in the wilderness."

When we face insurmountable odds, it is so easy to lose our perspective over the situation. Too often when we are confronted with an impossible situation, rather than meet it head on, we want to take the easy way out. We say, "I don't want to face this; I don't want to have to fight so I'll just go back to Egypt and resume my life as a slave."

It may be that this very day, someone hearing these words is thinking… "If God doesn't take this pressure off, I am going back to my old life." It may seem like it at this moment, but a full slave is much worse off than a hungry free man. Freedom to walk with God brings possibilities. Slavery to sin brings death – God's Word could not be more clear! The people in the narrative didn't have all that we have, so don't be too hard on them!

They weren't separated - Not all the company were Israelites. Exodus 12:38 revealed that a "mixed multitude came out of Egypt with Israel."

They had no Word - Israel had not written scripture at this point in their history to turn to.

They had no pattern of freedom - As slaves they had always lived at the edge of subsistence and were easily given to fear. The text says the Israelites were not just afraid, they were "very" afraid, and I believe that even that does not do justice to the terror they felt.

Choose to walk obediently while leaving the running of the universe to God. If God's purpose is to use us as a testimony, we don't have to fix everything. God will do what God needs done if we give His Word as instructed (14:13-15).

Exodus 14:13 But Moses said to the people, "Do not fear! Stand by and see the salvation of the LORD which He will accomplish for you today; for the Egyptians whom you have seen today, you will never see them again forever. 14 The LORD will fight for you while you keep silent." 15 Then the LORD said to Moses, "Why are you crying out to Me? Tell the sons of Israel to go forward."

God's instructions through Moses are four-fold.

- **"Fear Not."** He instructed the people first of all not to be afraid.

- **"Stand Still"** might be better understood to say, "Stand firm" – reflecting faith and confidence in the delivering power of Jehovah.

- **"Watch"** – Moses says, "See… what the Lord will accomplish for you today." God does not need your help. You don't need to fight, you need to stay out of the way. Just watch Him work.

- **Keep silent** – "Hold your peace." Often the hardest for us to do is this, because we feel that we just have to tell somebody about the predicament that we are in. But the only one who can do anything about our predicament already knows. He is waiting for us to look to him and be silent. All of these instructions are directed to natural human responses to panic.

First, we are afraid. Second, we run. Third, we fight. Fourth, we tell everyone who will listen.

Choose to courageously face that God's purposes are bigger than we can grasp, and He will, no doubt, call you to do things well beyond your ability. (14:16-18).

Exodus 14:16 As for you, lift up your staff and stretch out your hand over the sea and divide it, and the sons of Israel shall go through the midst of the sea on dry land. 17 As for Me, behold, I will harden the hearts of the Egyptians so that they will go in after them; and I will be honored through Pharaoh and all his army, through his chariots and his horsemen. 18 Then the Egyptians will know that I am the LORD, when I am honored through Pharaoh, through his chariots and his horsemen.

Pastor John Hamby wrote: "Nine year old Joey was asked by his mother what he had learned in Sunday School that day. 'Well, Mom, our teacher told us how God sent Moses behind the enemy lines on a rescue mission to lead the Israelites out of Egypt. When he got to the Red Sea, he had his engineers build a pontoon bridge, and all the people walked across safely. He used his walkie-talkie to radio headquarters and call in an air strike. They sent in bombers to blow up the bridge and all the Israelites were saved.' 'Now, Joey, is that REALLY what your teacher taught you?' his mother asked. 'Well, no, Mom, but if I told it the way the teacher did, you'd never believe it!'"

Choose to accept that God owes you no complete explanation of how He intends to work. God defends His work in ways that may look like they make no sense to you or the people around you! (14:19).

Mature vessels will learn to see God's hand in what is happening and learn to discern some of the purposes! (14:20). God works well **beyond our list of possibilities**! (14:21-22)

Exodus 14:19 The angel of God, who had been going before the camp of Israel, moved and went behind them; and the pillar of cloud moved from before them and stood behind them. 20 So it came between the camp of Egypt and the camp of Israel; and there was the cloud along with the darkness, yet it gave light at night. Thus the one did not come near the other all night. 21 Then Moses stretched out his hand over the sea; and the LORD swept the sea back by a strong east wind all night and turned the sea into dry land, so the waters were divided. 22 The sons of Israel went through the midst of the sea on the dry land, and the waters were like a wall to them on their right hand and on their left.

Choose to warn yourself often that we follow God to be used of God. Remember life without God is more difficult than it appears. People who think they can participate in the power of God without the purposes of God are badly mistaken (14:23-25).

Exodus 14:23 Then the Egyptians took up the pursuit, and all Pharaoh's horses, his chariots and his horsemen went in after them into the midst of the sea. 24 At the morning watch, the LORD looked down on the army of the Egyptians through the pillar of fire and cloud and brought the army of the Egyptians into confusion. 25 He caused their chariot wheels to swerve, and He made them drive with difficulty; so the Egyptians said, "Let us flee from Israel, for the LORD is fighting for them against the Egyptians."

"It may be that you have developed a rather materialistic lifestyle. Like Moses, and the children of Israel you have rubbed shoulders with folks in Egypt most of your life. You work with Egyptians. Think like Egyptians. Read Egyptian newspapers. Listen to Egyptian music. Do commercial battles with Egyptian entrepreneurs. You're in the competitive world of the Egyptians, so it's only natural that you react like them." (Charles Swindoll. *Moses: A Man of Selfless Devotion,* Nashville: Word Publishing, 1999 p. 223)

Choose to accept that God is a righteous judge. It is our privilege to be used by God's hand to show His power to the world (14:26-29).

Exodus 14:26 Then the LORD said to Moses, "Stretch out your hand over the sea so that the waters may come back over the Egyptians, over their chariots and their horsemen." 27 So Moses stretched out his hand over the sea, and the sea returned to its normal state at daybreak, while the Egyptians were fleeing right into it; then the LORD overthrew the Egyptians in the midst of the sea. 28 The waters returned and covered the chariots and the horsemen, even Pharaoh's entire army that had gone into the sea after them; not even one of them remained. 29 But the sons of Israel walked on dry land through the midst of the sea, and the waters were like a wall to them on their right hand and on their left.

Choose to identify God's hand of blessing on your life. When God acts and His people see Him clearly, they see the world for what it is (14:30).

We need to rehearse the blessings twice what we say about our dislikes and troubles, because they are more easily forgotten!

Exodus 14:30 Thus the LORD saved Israel that day from the hand of the Egyptians, and Israel saw the Egyptians dead on the seashore.

Choose to accept the truth that the troubles are worth it all, for God will show Himself and be praised! (14:31).

Exodus 14: 31 When Israel saw the great power which the LORD had used against the Egyptians, the people feared the LORD, and they believed in the LORD and in His servant Moses.

Your future may seem impossible, and the problems impassable – but God is working a plan. You are where you are because God has something He can teach you.

"Often God seems to place His children in positions of profound difficulty, leading them into a wedge from which there is no escape, designing a situation that no human judgment would have permitted had it been previously consulted. The very cloud directs them there. You..., may be involved in a situation like this at this very hour. It does seem perplexing and mysterious to the last degree, but it is perfectly right. The issue will more than justify Him who has brought you there. It is a platform for the display of His almighty grace and power. Not only will He deliver you, but in doing so He will give you a lesson that you will never forget ...." (F.B. Meyer. *The Life of Moses: The Servant of God*, Lynnwood, Washington: Emerald Books, 1996.0 p. 80)

To become a vessel God can use, I must understand and live the choices that will honor God.

The Message offers this note to close from 2 Timothy 2:20ff: In a well-furnished kitchen there are not only crystal goblets and silver platters, but waste cans and compost buckets—some containers used to serve fine meals, others to take out the garbage. Become the kind of container God can use to present any and every kind of gift to his guests for their blessing. Run away from infantile indulgence. Run after mature righteousness—faith, love, peace — joining those who are in honest and serious prayer before God. Refuse to get involved in inane discussions; they always end up in fights. God's servant must not be argumentative, but a gentle listener and a teacher who keeps cool, working firmly but patiently with those who refuse to obey. You never know how or when God might sober them up with a change of heart and a turning to the truth, enabling them to escape the Devil's trap, where they are caught and held captive, forced to run his errands.

Grasping God's Purpose: Lessons in Exodus

Lesson Fourteen: Exodus 15:1-27 "The Day after Syndrome"

There we stood; there was not a single dry eye in the place. We had been up until all hours of the night every day of the last week. We were all saying "Goodbye" tomorrow. How had we grown so close together in just one week? Pastor Ed had just preached about giving our all to Jesus. We were all sure we would be ready to read our Bible no less than daily, and reach our entire school for Christ. We were the committed, the empowered. We were kids on a mission. Our lives would never be the same. We surrendered great things – such great things as can be surrendered by elementary school boys. What a time of worship we had! The sticks were tossed on the fire as we symbolically told Jesus we were ready to live for Him in all things. We were ready for anything… anything, that is, but going home, anything - but living these truths when we got home.

Don't get me wrong; our hearts were emotionally immature, but our feelings were absolutely genuine. We believed what we were saying. The plateau we reached in our elementary school walk was not false… it was just set in an unreal setting. Life would set in and test our resolve. Long after camp, at least a few weeks or so, we would struggle to live the ideals we swore to at the campfire. Was the time wasted? I don't believe so. Even in the camp experience of plateaus, our fragile and infant faith was being nurtured. We did leave stronger than we came in. We needed the experience of the "Rise and Fall" that followed as part of our growing process…

Have you ever left a worship time with the Lord elated, excited, committed and joyful – only to have it all come crashing down on your head? Have you ever seriously committed things to the Lord in a special time of consecration? Maybe it was a promise in a hospital room. Maybe it was a praise moment after a deliverance of the Lord. Looking back, you were genuine in your surrender, but what followed was unforeseen in your life. Everything seemed like it was even worse than before. You really thought you were going to be able to walk with God… but in a blink the whole dream soured. Problems rushed in and nothing worked. If you know what that is like, this passage is for you.

Like a play with a "split stage," Exodus 15 has two very different and even contrasting scenes. The first was elation and worship; the second was the "day after" when a pummeling of problems rolled in. It is a natural experience for us – for we live in two realms at the same time. The joys of the world above don't cancel the power of the problems below. Yet, Intimacy with God gives us strength to care for BOTH worlds at the same time!

Key Principle: I must learn Who God is and how He works in the journey to be able to both enjoy life and walk with Him.

In order to understand the problem of the second half, let's spend a few minutes in the joy of the Hot Hit in the first half of the passage…

The "Song of Preparation" for the Journey (Exodus 15:1-21)

Exodus 15:1 Then Moses and the sons of Israel sang this song to the LORD, and said, "I will sing to the LORD, for He is highly exalted; the horse and its rider He has hurled into the sea. 2 The LORD is my strength and song, and He has become my salvation; this is my God, and I will praise Him; my father's God, and I will extol Him. 3 The LORD is a warrior; the LORD is His name. 4 Pharaoh's chariots and his army He has cast into the sea; and the choicest of his officers are drowned in the Red Sea. 5 The deeps cover them; they went down into the depths like a stone. 6 Your right hand, O LORD, is majestic in power; Your right hand, O LORD, shatters the enemy. 7 And in the greatness of Your excellence You overthrow those who rise up against You; You send forth Your burning anger, and it consumes them as chaff. 8 At the blast of Your nostrils the waters were piled up; the flowing waters stood up like a heap; the deeps were congealed in the heart of the sea. 9 The enemy said, 'I will pursue, I will overtake, I will divide the spoil; my desire shall be gratified against them; I will draw out my sword, my hand will destroy them.' 10 "You blew with Your wind, the sea covered them; they sank like lead in the mighty waters. 11 Who is like You among the gods, O LORD? Who is like You, majestic in holiness, awesome in praises, working wonders? 12 You stretched out Your right hand, the earth swallowed them. 13 In Your lovingkindness You have led the people whom You have redeemed; in Your strength You have guided them to Your holy habitation. 14 The peoples have heard; they tremble; anguish has gripped the inhabitants of Philistia. 15 Then the chiefs of Edom were dismayed, the leaders of Moab; trembling grips them; all the inhabitants of Canaan have melted away. 16 Terror and dread fall upon them; by the greatness of Your arm they are motionless as stone until Your people pass over, O LORD, until the people pass over whom You have purchased. 17 You will bring them and plant them in the mountain of Your inheritance, the place, O LORD, which You have made for Your dwelling, the sanctuary, O Lord, which Your hands have established. 18 The LORD shall reign forever and ever." 19 For the horses of Pharaoh with his chariots and his horsemen went into the sea, and the LORD brought back the waters of the sea on them, but the sons of Israel walked on dry land through the midst of the sea. 20 Miriam the prophetess, Aaron's sister, took the timbrel in her hand, and all the women went out after her with timbrels and with dancing. 21 Miriam answered them, "Sing to the LORD, for He is highly exalted; the horse and his rider He has hurled into the sea."

Moses led a song with the people: This is now a famous song sung in synagogues around the world on Shabbat. Later it will become a part of the song of the redeemed Jewish people that add to it the song of the Lamb in Revelation 15:3 in Heaven!

Refrain: Who is like You? (15:11)

Mi-chamochah b'elem Adonai (YHWH): Who is like You among the gods, O LORD? Mi-chamochah ne-adar b'kodesh: Who is like You glorified in holiness? Nora t'hiloth oseh feleh - oseh feleh: Fearful/Revered in praises; Worker of Wonders!

Don't skip the details. The song was:

Directed to the Lord (1): *Exodus 15:1a Then Moses and the sons of Israel sang this song to the LORD, and said…"*

Redemption is impossible without God, and the redeemed need to turn back to God and PRAISE Him and thank Him for the great thing He has done. We praise Him when He delivers our body from harm. We praise when He heals from sickness. Which is harder, to say "rise up and walk" or to say "your sins are forgiven you"? Tell the Lord you want to PRAISE HIM for accomplishing your new life.

Once the song was lifted, the contents yielded **important truths** about God:

Exodus 15:1b: …I will sing to the LORD, for He is highly exalted; The horse and its rider He has hurled into the sea.

Truth 1: God has His place (15:1b "Lord" is Master)

I am overjoyed to call Him my Master. He has all rights to my life, my happiness, my fulfillment!

Truth 2: God holds His position (15:1b: "exalted")

I will not lift another above Him in my eyes or my heart, He is first!

Truth 3: God does His powerful work (151b: "hurled")

There is NOTHING He can't do to defend me. He can pull apart the Earth itself to hold on to me!

Exodus 15:2 The LORD is my strength and song, and He has become my salvation; this is my God, and I will praise Him; my father's God, and I will extol Him. 3 The LORD is a warrior; the LORD is His name. 4 Pharaoh's chariots and his army He has cast into the sea; and the choicest of his officers are drowned in the Red Sea. 5 The deeps cover them; they went down into the depths like a stone.

Before you move on, notice the description of Moses relationship with God, and listen to how excited he was to walk with God:

The relationship with God was **Personal** (15:2 "my"): He is the object of my praise and worship! It was **Empowering** (15:2 "strength"): He gives me the power to keep going! It was **Joyful** (15:2b "my song"): He fills my mouth with song and my heart with joy! He felt **Rescued** (15:2b "my salvation"): He threw a lifeline to me when no one else will! He felt **Defended** (15:2b "Elohim"): He stands over me to defend me in strength! He felt **Connected** (15:2b "my Father's God"): He bonds me to a history of His legacy! He appeared as **Victorious** (15:3-5; 19 "warrior" mentioned and then illustrated): When I am overwhelmed, He is there to create a victory over my enemy!

In Moses life, God showed Himself through His performance – He related through His "working features" (15:6-13):

Take for example the expression of His "right hand" (6-7): Majestic, shattering power that consumes those who stand against You.

Exodus 15:6 Your right hand, O LORD, is majestic in power, Your right hand, O LORD, shatters the enemy. 7 And in the greatness of Your excellence You overthrow those who rise up against You; You send forth Your burning anger, and it consumes them as chaff.

Later the Right Hand is mentioned again (12-13): The sign to all creation to obey, it swallowed enemies and led us gently at the same time!

Exodus 15:12 You stretched out Your right hand, The earth swallowed them. 13 In Your lovingkindness You have led the people whom You have redeemed; In Your strength You have guided them to Your holy habitation.

Look at the notice Moses took of God's "nostrils" (8-10): They were a powerful force that drove back the sea and shut down the pursuit of the enemy.

Exodus 15:8 At the blast of Your nostrils the waters were piled up, the flowing waters stood up like a heap; the deeps were congealed in the heart of the sea. 9 The enemy said, "I will pursue; I will overtake, I will divide the spoil." My desire shall be gratified against them; I will draw out my sword, my hand will destroy them. 10 You blew with Your wind, the sea covered them; they sank like lead in the mighty waters.

God worked according to His purposes (Exodus 15:14-19)

He wanted to let the **world know** of Him (15:14-15): He wanted all Creation to know of Him!

Exodus 14 The peoples have heard; they tremble; anguish has gripped the inhabitants of Philistia. 15 Then the chiefs of Edom were dismayed; the leaders of Moab, trembling grips them; all the inhabitants of Canaan have melted away.

He desired to let His **redeemed be rescued** (15:16-17a): He wanted His people to acknowledge His rescue!

Exodus 15:16 Terror and dread fall upon them; by the greatness of Your arm they are motionless as stone; until Your people pass over, O LORD, until the people pass over whom You have purchased

He made it possible for **worship of Him to be established** (15:17b): He wanted to be at the center of the hearts of His people!

Exodus 15:17 You will bring them and plant them in the mountain of Your inheritance, the place, O LORD, which You have made for Your dwelling, the sanctuary, O Lord, which Your hands have established.

He wanted His **sovereign control to be known** (15:18): He wanted to bring about the righteous rule He promised!

Exodus 15:18 The LORD shall reign forever and ever.

Here again, the refrain would be sung…

Mi-chamochah b'elem Adonai (YHWH): Who is like You among the gods, O LORD? *Mi-chamochah ne-adar b'kodesh:* Who is like You *glorified in holiness*? *Nora t'hiloth oseh feleh - oseh feleh:* Fearful or revered in praises; Worker of Wonders!

Stop! See what the Lord revealed about Himself through His servant Moses in a moment of joy!

It was the pattern of preparation for **hardship**! The song is again sung in human history. The stage is set in Revelation 15:3. In the shadow of the Great Throne of God the sound of the voices of Jewish martyrs begin to cry out. From the anguish of their life on Earth they were forcibly born into the presence of the Holy One, even as a newborn baby is pushed into arrival. Entering Heaven with tear-filled eyes, God wipes their eyes and pulls them to His side. "Well done, My child!" says the Master.

Almost without thought they begin to sing the words they have learned from their youth. These Jewish followers of Jesus cry out, *Mi-chamochah b'elem Adonai* (YHWH): Who is like You among the gods, O LORD?

Mi-chamochah ne-adar b'kodesh: Who is like You glorified in holiness? ***Nora t'hiloth oseh feleh - oseh feleh*:** Fearful/revered in praises; Worker of wonders!

What are these words they sing? What are they saying?

They are affirming aloud: "My God is My Master! He has my heart and is exalted in my eyes! He stops at NOTHING to cling to me, and holds me in His hand! He gives me the power to make it through troubles and the joy to fill my heart in the journey! He rescues me from the pit of despair and stands as a strong defender over my life. He connects me to the great drama of history – His story.

He makes me a victor over the enemies of discouragement, addiction, and a broken life. With His great right hand He orders the worlds; all Creation is formed and crushed in His hands. With a mere breathe He shuts down any enemy that pursues me, and uses His hand to gently lead me. He wants the world to know Him, and He desires to rescue even more of my world! He hungers that we would enjoy Him, for He knows that only when I recognize His greatness and love Him intimately will I truly find fulfillment! Great is our God! Great is Our God!"

In Exodus 15, the excitement receded, and what replaced the celebration was…heat and trouble. Salvation is exciting; the Christian life can be just plain hard. That's the truth. Obedience and surrender are right and biblical and really, really tough. If anyone tells you otherwise, they are lying. It is worth it, but it is hard.

Lessons of Living on the Journey (15:22-27)

Follow the progression of the story in *Exodus 15:22 Then Moses led Israel from the Red Sea, and they went out into the wilderness of Shur; and they went three days in the wilderness and found no water. 23 When they came to Marah, they could not drink the waters of Marah, for they were bitter; therefore, it was named Marah. 24 So the people grumbled at Moses, saying, "What shall we drink?" 25 Then he cried out to the LORD, and the LORD showed him a tree; and he threw it into the waters, and the waters became sweet. There He made for them a statute and regulation, and there He tested them. 26 And He said, "If you will give earnest heed to the voice of the LORD your God, and do what is right in His sight, and give ear to His commandments, and keep all His statutes, I will put none of the diseases on you which I have put on the Egyptians; for I, the LORD, am your healer." 27 Then they came to Elim where there were twelve springs of water and seventy date palms, and they camped there beside the waters.*

Seven Lessons for the Journey:

Lesson One: The Departure Lesson- Moses led them from the place of victory to the desert, and the people began to suffer (15:22).

Exodus 15:22 Then Moses led Israel from the Red Sea, and they went out into the wilderness of Shur; and they went three days in the wilderness and found no water.

We must move back from the place of celebration to the problems that we face in our lives. The worship is designed to strengthen us and give us hunger for God, not a place to hide from our problems!

"In November of 1988 a 19 year old woman fell asleep behind the wheel of her car at about 2:15 in the morning. Her car plunged thru a guardrail and was dangling by its left rear tire. A half dozen passing motorists stopped, grabbed some ropes from one of their vehicles tied the ropes to the back of her car, & hung on until fire units arrived. A ladder was extended from below to help stabilize the car while firefighters tied the vehicle to tow trucks with cables and chains. One of the rescuers later said, 'Every time we would move the car, she would yell and scream. She was in terrible pain.' For nearly 2 ½ hours police officers, tow truck drivers, firefighters and passers-by (about 25 people in all)worked to secure the car and pull the woman to safety. All through the episode, the woman kept repeated a phrase over and over to rescuers. She kept saying: 'I'll do it myself.'" (November 20, 1988, the *Los Angeles Times*)

This woman was in horrible pain. She was pinned inside her car, and she was unable to change her circumstances or save herself from her danger. Ultimately, it took the efforts of nearly 25 people to rescue her from potential death -- and yet, she kept thinking she could solve the problem all by herself.

Lesson Two: The Disappointment Lesson- When they finally got to a place with water, they found that drinking the water made them ill (15:23).

Exodus 15:23 When they came to Marah, they could not drink the waters of Marah, for they were bitter; therefore it was named Marah.

"The contrast between the great time with God and the reality of life here can be painful." (cp. *Elijah*).

There is nothing wrong; that is the way life is, and we should expect it. "They could not drink" can be translated they *could not bear to drink* (elo yakoli).

Lesson Three: The Dissention Lesson- What do we do now? (15:24)

Exodus 15:24: So the people grumbled at Moses, saying, "What shall we drink?"

Voices that were quick to celebrate will be equally quick to complain!

Lesson Four: The Deliverance Lesson- Moses cried to the Lord and the Lord directed him to cast a tree limb into the water to make it potable without any ill effects (15:25a).

Exodus 15:25 Then he cried out to the LORD, and the LORD showed him a tree; and he threw it into the waters, and the waters became sweet….

God provided a way of escape after they failed to drink water that would make them ill.

Deliverance often includes doing something that requires discipline and obedience – it wasn't intended to be easy.

Lesson Five: The Detail Lesson- The whole thing was a test from God (15:25b).

Exodus 15:25b …There He made for them a statute and regulation, and there He tested them.

God wanted to help them by making them sick, and getting the parasites of Egypt from them. If we simply obey right down to the detail, it may seem more painful up front, but it is the best way to get through the wilderness!

They say "the devil is in the details!" The story is told of a little boy who went to the grocery store and asked the clerk for a box of laundry detergent. The clerk was very impressed at such a little guy taking on the responsibilities of helping his mom with the household chores. So he said to the boy "Well that is mighty grown up of you to be willing to help your mother out with the washing." Well the little guy wanted to set the record straight so he told the clerk, "Oh, I'm not going to use it to wash clothes, I need it for my dog." The clerk was a little concerned at that point and so he said "Don't you think this detergent might be a little strong for washing a dog?" The little boy replied, "Well, that's what I want, he's a mighty dirty dog." So the boy took the box of detergent home, and about a week later returned. Well the clerk recognized him and asked him about his dog. The little boy said, "O my dog is dead!" The clerk was shocked. "Oh that's so terrible. I guess that laundry detergent was too strong after all." The little boy thought for a minute and said "No, I don't think it was the detergent that got him, I think it was the rinse cycle."

Have you ever gone through a time in your life when you felt like you had been through the wringer?

Lesson Six: The Directive Lesson- God told them, "Next time do what I say, even if you think it will make you sick; I am working a plan!" (15:26).

Exodus 15:26 And He said, "If you will give earnest heed to the voice of the LORD your God, and do what is right in His sight, and give ear to His commandments, and keep all His statutes, I will put none of the diseases on you which I have put on the Egyptians; for I, the LORD, am your healer."

God knows what He is asking, and why! He is the healer!

The test is not whether or not God is true, but whether or not I will believe and follow.

Lesson Seven: The Down Time Lesson

Exodus 15:27 Then they came to Elim where there were twelve springs of water and seventy date palms, and they camped there beside the waters.

They arrived at a place of rest, with fresh water and no test. Many people get to Marah and never leave. They won't go on to Elim; they sit in bitterness and wallow. God is His goodness gave them an escape and they were all able to continue. The way out of the wilderness is through it! The Bible doesn't leave us in the dark as to Who God is and what He is like.

"Apparently, in New Hampshire, a man named Josh Muszynski stopped at a gas station and bought a pack of cigarettes with his debit card. A few hours later, he was online checking his bank account and found that this particular pack of cigarettes set him back: $23,148,855,308,184,500.00. That's 23 quadrillion, 148 trillion, 855 billion, 308 million, 184 thousand, 500 dollars. To put that in perspective: if you took all the money from all the countries in the United Nations, you still wouldn't have enough money to buy that single pack of cigarettes. Needless to say, Josh immediately called his bank and managed to clear things up. Not only did his bank correct the error, they also removed the $15 overdraft fee they charged him." (Patrick D. Odum, Heartlight.org 8/11/09)

The point is: If this man had actually owed that much money there was no way he (or anyone else on face of Earth) could ever pay it back.

They should have understood from their time of worship: **When I truly understand Who God is I can face a trouble filled life here and now with confidence!**

www.ingramcontent.com/pod-product-compliance
Lightning Source LLC
Chambersburg PA
CBHW061723020426
42331CB00006B/1071

9780692291214